THE TONGUE OF A TEACHER

THE HISTORICAL SERIES OF THE REFORMED CHURCH IN AMERICA
NO. 103

THE TONGUE OF A TEACHER
Essays in Honor of the Rev. Dr. Timothy Brown

Edited by Trygve D. Johnson

REFORMED CHURCH PRESS
Grand Rapids, Michigan

Printed in the United States of America

ISBN: 978-1-950572-17-5

Library of Congress Control Number: 2021938405

Donors

We extend appreciation to the following people for generously supporting the publishing of this volume

First Reformed Church,
South Holland, IL
Eddy & Daysi Aleman
Marv & Sue Andringa
Richard & Shelly Arnold
Brian & Christina Aulick
Marc & Patti Baer
Ron & Helen Bakker
Jeff & Karen Barker
Tom & Mary Bartha
Andy & Katie Bast
Peter & Sarah Bast
Ken & Mary Bauman
Michael & Erin Beckerink
Mike & Elaine Becksvoort
Tim & Marta Belstra
Bob & Jennifer Bieri
Thomas & Linda Bock
Irv & Irene Boersen
Bill & Claire Boersma
Bryan & Melissa Boersma
Ryan & Megan Boes
Mike & Tena Bos
Rick & Barb Boss
Bob & Barbara Bredeweg
Linda Breen
John & Marylin Bright
Jerry & Jane Brown
Bill Brownson
Jon & Jeannette Brownson
James & Kathleen Hart Brumm
Jim & Martie Bultman
Austin & Kathryn Campbell
William & Sandra Church
Dan & Grace Claus
Megan Dalman
Wilbur Daniels
Matthew & Alissa Davis
Mark & Kay DeCook
Steve & JoAnn DeCook
Peter & Elka Deede
Ron & Rebecca Deering
Martin & Lorraine DeHaan
Phil & Rosalyn DeKoster
Ted & Ellen DeLong
John & Ann DenHartog
Esther DePree
Mark DeRoo
Herb & Kate Dershem
Lee & Linda DeVisser
Marilyn DeVree
Ron & Nell DeVree
Don & Minnie DeWitt
Gary & Joyce DeWitt
Mary DeWitt
Merle & Sheri DeWitt
Tim & Brenda Dieffenbach
Karl & Lori Droppers
Kurt & Leah Dykstra
Al & Marcia Elgersma
Jonathan & Kendra Elgersma
Hennie Elsinga
Ken & Terry Elzinga
Mark Eriks
Ted & Barb Etheridge
John Everts
Newton & Vicky Fairweather
Chuck & Thelma Ferguson
Matt & Marcia Floding
Bruce & Susan Formsma

Percy & Shireen Gilbert
William & Andrea Godwin-Stremler
Rick & Lani Gorzeman
Joe & Tiffany Graham
Dan & Jan Harris
Ken Harris
Harmen & Grace Heeg
Dennis & Lynne Hendricks
James & Janet Herrick
Etta Hesselink
Rob & Jeannie Hilarides
Joanne Hoffman
Taylor & Cathy Holbrook
Bill & Jeanine Holman
Dave & Leslie Hooker
Rob & Shanna Housman
Roger & Charlotte Huitink
Heidi Huizenga
Dave & Kristin Izenbart
Donald & Ina Jansen
Jim & Candy Jeltema
David & Arlene Johnson
Trygve & Kristen Johnson
Bruce & Margie Johnson
Fred Johnson, III
Jim Jurries
Andy & Samantha Kadzban
Jim Kaminski
Brian & Tammy Keepers
Larry & Christine Kieft
John & Sharon Kleinheksel
Paul & Jacki Kleinheksel
Elsie Kloote
Harry & Diane Konynenbelt
Brian & Cathy Koop
Darrell & Debra Koopmans
Cor Kors
John & Gay Kraai
Andrea Kragt
Kelvin & Ellen Kronemeyer
Fritz & Sharon Kruithof
Aaron & Kerri Kuecker
Rich & Sue Kuiper
Charles & Bea Kulier
Arlyn & Marcia Lanting
Jim & Lori LeFebre
Matt & Sarah LeFebre
Jim & Barb Lester
Jeanne Lindell
Rick & Mary Lyons
Marge Maas
Jul & Jackie Medenblik
John & Linda Moons
Bud & Joyce Mouw
Richard & Phyllis Mouw
Fred Mueller
Larry & Karen Mulder
Jim & Judy Nace
Rex & Sheri Nederend
Gary & Peggy Nielsen
Jerry & Cheryl Nienhuis
John & Nancy Norden
Tom & Marilyn Norman
Cyndi Nykamp
Erma Nykamp
Jon & Ann Opgenorth
Adam & Julie Paarlberg
Tom & Fonda Paarlberg
Irma Patterson
Eric & Elizabeth Peterson
Steve & Monica Pierce
Cornelius & Kathy Plantinga
Ann Plas
Mark & Jean Poppen
Tom & Gloria Pratt
Perry & Cherie Raak
Jerry & Elsie Redeker
Pat Riarkey
Rob & Rebecca Riekse
Dan & Cathy Rink
David & Jennifer Ryden
Cal & Marilyn Rynbrandt
James & Catherine Schoon
Tom & Grace Schwanda
Norm & Terry Schuiling

Matt & Sarah Scoggin
Stephen & Olga Shaffer
Dorothy Sherburne
Tim & Charley Shotmeyer
John & Betty Sikkink
Steve & Carol Simon
Ted & Jackie Simpkins
Jerry & Patricia Sittser
Ray & Sue Smith
Jamie K.A. Smith
Beth Snyder
Samuel Solivan
John & Judy Spoelhof
Steve & Valerie Spoelhof
Vern & Carla Sterk
Bob & Deborah Sterken
Doug & Dee Dee Stewart
Doug & Vicky Struyk
J.P. & Katy Sundararajan
Ryan & Jaclyn Sweet
Norm & Melita Swier
Cora Taitt
Dave & Sally Tapley
Brian & Becky Telzerow
Timothy & Julie Tennent
Tiger & Shirley Teusink
Felix & Esther Theonugraha
Christopher & Arika VanDam
Steve & Mieneke Thomas
Tom Thomas
Don & Coralynne Van'tHof
Wayne & Jill VanDam
Lee & Nancy VandeBunte
Paul & Kathleen VandenBrink
Stan & Mary VandenBrink
Al & Lenore VanderMeer
Jim VanderMeiden
Ted & Joan Vanderveen
Dar & Kathleen VanderWal
David & Lisa VanderWal
Jeffrey & Amy VanDrunen
Art & Beatrice VanEck
Chuck & Jean VanEngen
Phyllis VanLandegent
Josh & Heather VanLeeuwen
Scott VanRavenswaay
Judy VanRees
Clare & Joan VanWieren
Jim & Wanda Veld
Terry & Cindi Veldheer DeYoung
Dave & Ellen Vellenga
Sid & Carol Verdoorn
Evan & Nancy Vermeer
Shane & Jill VerSteeg
Lynn & Mary Vincent
Drew & Jean Vogel
John & Mary Voorn
Dennis & Betty Lou Voskuil
Matt & Sarah Waterstone
Steve & Martha Wing
Roger & Wilma Winkels
Ron & Sherrie Wolthuis
Jerry & Mary Zwart

The Historical Series of the Reformed Church in America

The series was inaugurated in 1968 by the General Synod of the Reformed Church in America acting through the Commission on History to communicate the church's heritage and collective memory and to reflect on our identity and mission, encouraging historical scholarship which informs both church and academy.

www.rca.org/series

Contents

Foreword

Leanne Van Dyk

It is never easy to be a seminary president; that much is sure. The day-to-day pressures of budgets and regulations and donors and personnel are unrelenting. But Timothy Brown, president of Western Theological Seminary (WTS) from 2008 to 2019, carried these expected pressures with dignity, steady patience, and robust collegiality. His presidency was marked not only by these typical leadership pressures but also by at least two other heavy burdens that tested him.

First, the well-documented period of decline and contraction in mainline denominations nationally has directly impacted theological education, including at Western, in multiple ways. A November 2016 report from the Pew Research Center had the intriguing title "If the U.S. had 100 people: Charting Americans' religious beliefs and practices." Using that rubric of 100 people, America would have 23 religiously unaffiliated people, 25 self-identified evangelicals, and 15 mainline Christians. The remaining 37 persons would represent Roman Catholics and other faith traditions. This striking picture illustrates the dramatic decline in religious affiliation in America in the last few decades, a decline that presses in on denominational leaders, congregational pastors, and seminary presidents.

An obvious result of the decline that Pew reports is lower seminary student enrollment. This is a difficult reality to accept, and it requires wise adjustments while still pursuing the mission of the seminary. A decline in donor gifts and other revenue sources is also a marker of denominational decline with direct impact on the life of the seminary.

The second heavy burden that fell on Tim was a time of painful and divisive controversies in the Reformed Church in America (RCA). Heated and seemingly entrenched polemics marked Tim's presidency and continue during the current administration. The seminary was urged by some to advocate one line of thought and by others to advocate the exact opposite. Certainly, this kind of dynamic puts enormous pressure on the seminary president. But Tim's commitment was not to "take sides" but to both model and train seminarians to respond faithfully, wisely, and effectively in the context of these controversies.

Even in the face of these daunting obstacles, Tim Brown approached his call to serve as president of Western with uncommon optimism, humor, and fairness. Among all his other accomplishments, this posture of joy and steady positivity marked his presidency through both sunny successes as well as stormy tests of courage and faith.

I served as the dean for much of Tim's eleven years as president, so I saw his leadership from the inside. He chaired the President's Council, which is the executive team comprising the president, the four vice presidents, and the executive assistant to the president. Each week, he would open with the meeting with a reading from Scripture or a devotional classic (John Bunyan's *The Pilgrim's Progress* was one of his favorites, as was Dietrich Bonhoeffer's *Life Together*). It was clear to us around his conference table that he placed his leadership call squarely in the framework of his faith and that he expected us to do the same. Those executive meetings were often marked by hearty laughter and inside jokes. Occasionally, they included sharp disagreement and debate. But even on those days, the umbrella of our shared faith commitments protected our collegiality and our partnership.

The timeline of Tim Brown's presidency at WTS is marked by two significant bookends. At the beginning of his presidency, the dramatic renovation of Mulder Chapel was accomplished, and at the end of his presidency, the equally dramatic renovation of the library, administrative offices, and learning spaces was celebrated. Tim put his whole heart and soul into both of those important projects, and each represents one of his core commitments in theological education.

The first commitment I would like to identify was apparent throughout Tim's presidency but can be seen most clearly in the chapel renovation. That commitment was to amplify the full beauty and strength of Reformed worship. The chapel was designed with the explicit insights of Reformed theology in mind, including the sacramental significance of light and shape, scriptural centrality (seen not only in pulpit but also in stained glass), Trinitarian references, and a contemporary expression of the beauty of God. Beauty and sacrament are not always on the "top ten" list of Reformed theological emphases, but at Western, under Tim's leadership and with the collaboration of the faculty, these Reformed insights were refreshed and highlighted. The renovated chapel has served for more than a decade now in deeply shaping the spirituality and theological formation of students, faculty, and staff. It is a holy space, and it emerged from the vision of a skilled architect, a creative faculty committee, and a determined president. The legacy of the seminary chapel is one of the lasting impacts of Timothy Brown's leadership.

The second bookend of Tim's presidency, the renovation of the library and other spaces, represents the other primary commitment of his presidency: a full endorsement of the classic Reformed emphasis on an educated clergy. It is certainly the case that the old 1955 building needed an update, but Tim's strong support of the design and funding for the project grew from a sturdy theological taproot, not merely from the vagaries of ventilation systems, old plumbing, and leaky roofs.

A commitment to a Reformed educated clergy and a hearty respect for the life of the mind prompted Tim to fully support the rigors of scholarship in service of the church. At a time of cynical anti-intellectualism in both our political and ecclesial cultures, Tim regularly promoted scholarship, its demands, and its potential to nourish faith and discipleship. Tim also understood the rapid rise of educational technology and therefore supported a library design that is better called a "learning center." The campus now bears visible witness to Tim's leadership at WTS and displays the confidence of significant donors in Tim's vision of theological education. Tim's presidency constitutes a noteworthy chapter in the story of the seminary.

That chapter of Tim's presidency at WTS will be articulated in the chapters of this book, commissioned to honor his accomplishments and commitments. The themes of this book mirror the themes of Tim's leadership at Western. His influence and encouragement to many students and colleagues were wide-ranging, and some of those people are honored to speak in these pages. Those themes include, most centrally, his commitment to compelling preaching deeply soaked in Scripture. But other themes have been demonstrated in his presidency as well, themes often concentrated in deep personal friendship. For example, Karen and Jeff Barker are longstanding friends who share Tim's awareness of the formational power of the arts, particularly the dramatic arts that Karen and Jeff have honed as they open up new vistas of biblical narratives in dramatic form. The relational ties in Nancy's and Tim's lives always nourished and informed Tim's leadership. His son, Jon Brown, writes of his dad as both a pastor and a parent, and eventually as a seminary president and a very proud grandparent. (Oh yes, the President's Council heard the stories of the grandchildren!) Other themes that emerged in Tim's leadership included an urgent call to racial justice and an affirmation of women in leadership. This latter affirmation is one that I myself noticed regularly and with deep gratitude.

It was an honor to serve as dean during Tim's presidency; I consider him a colleague, a mentor, and a friend. In my own present work as a seminary president, I learned key lessons from Timothy Brown. I learned to "absorb chaos and give back calm," as the leadership books instruct. I learned to seek consensus and welcome input. I learned to summon the courage to make hard decisions. I learned to extend thanks to colleagues, offer affirmation to students, and seek advice from trustees. I learned to articulate the vision and the mission again and yet again. I learned to enter each room, engage each conversation, confront each challenge from a core cluster of values and commitments. I congratulate Tim on an impressive list of accomplishments in his years as president and, even more, on the way he led from his whole heart. This, in my mind, is his signature accomplishment and, I believe, continues to motivate, instruct, and shape pastors and congregations who have been formed by Tim's life of faithful service.

Leanne Van Dyk
Columbia Theological Seminary
January 25, 2021

Preface

Leanne Van Dyk

This is a volume of essays created to honor the life, ministry, and legacy of the Rev. Dr. Timothy Brown. It is impossible, of course, to measure the significance of a life, or how one particular life has impacted so many others. But it is safe to say that Tim Brown's life created a ripple effect whose circumference reached far shores. He was many things to many people: a husband, a father, a friend, a theologian, a pastor, a preacher, a professor, a seminary president. But in these many roles, he never forgot his most primary identity: he was a child of God, he was a son of grace. His life and ministry helped thousands discover and sustain a faith where they lived into that identity for themselves.

Tim Brown was born in Battle Creek, Michigan, in 1951. But his beginning in this world was not without complication. It was this beginning that would later remind him to always look for and offer the grace of Christ to others in need. Tim was the son of Joyce Ann Lemmer. At the age of sixteen, she became involved with a young sailor on furlough and became pregnant and then married, but after eighteen months, Joyce left the marriage due to abuse. She had grown up in a strict Protestant Reformed church in Kalamazoo, where faith was defined by what you *didn't* do and discipline was experienced like a leather belt, and the young teenage mother was excommunicated from the church and shunned by her parents and church family. This drove a stake into her heart, and she vowed to never step foot in another church again.

Later, while working in a hardware store, Joyce met Richard (Dick) Brown, whose friends called him the "Iron Duke" since he carried himself with an imposing confidence. Joyce and Dick started to date, fell in love, and soon married, and Dick took on the responsibilities of a new family, becoming Dad to Tim's oldest sibling, Jim. Four more children were to come: Kathleen, Tim, Penny, and Kaye. Dick ran a construction company out of his home office (much like George Patton ran the Seventh Army Division in World War II), while Joyce dutifully kept the books and ran the home, raising Tim and his four siblings. Together they became a family, but never did they darken the door of a church together.

Tim grew up in Battle Creek. He was moderately interested in school and a successful student, but his imagination was captivated by sports. Playing and watching them was his passion. It was here, watching football games with his dad, that he became an avowed fan of the University of Michigan Wolverines—a passion that never faded. He graduated from Battle Creek Lakeview High School in the class of 1969. During the summer before his senior year, he met Hope College basketball coach Russ Devette, who saw Tim's size at a Hope basketball camp and invited him to try out for the Hope College basketball team. Having no other invitations to keep playing basketball, Tim enrolled as a freshman at Hope College with high hopes of furthering his athletic career. Tim's athletic career turned out to be a humble one. He was on the team, but he rode the bench most of the time. But he loved college, especially social life and the friends he made through his fraternity brothers.

During his freshman year (1969), while he was on a spring break trip with some of his pledge brothers in Daytona Beach, Florida, something happened to Tim that changed the trajectory of his life—and would affect the future of all those Tim would impact. One morning, while walking off a fuzzy head, Tim happened upon a band playing music. Tim stopped to listen. The band was made up of students working with Campus Crusade from the University of Georgia. The leader of the band started preaching. His witness was from 2 Corinthians 5:17: "So if anyone is in Christ, there is a new creation: everything old has passed away; see, everything has become new!" This simple message pierced Tim's heart and captured his imagination. In that moment, he felt the grip of Christ's grace seize and reorient his desire. He wanted to taste this fresh start. He desired to be a new creation. Right then and there, Tim Brown gave his life over to the lordship of Jesus Christ.

Tim returned to Hope a changed man. He identified as a Christian. His conversion was at one and the same time a conversion to Christian ministry. No longer did he have a desire to be a basketball coach—he was called to ministry. So Tim changed his major to Bible and religion. During this time, he also met a charismatic pastor named Dr. Bill Brownson, who was professor of preaching at Western Theological Seminary, and he began to disciple and encourage the newly christened Tim Brown into a vocation of Christian ministry.

While at Hope, he also met Nancy Johnson, and they dated. In 1971, the two were married. Tim graduated from Hope College in 1973. That same year, he enrolled at Western Theological Seminary (WTS) and began his preparation for pastoral ministry. He graduated from WTS in 1976, and that same year he was ordained into the Reformed Church in America (RCA) at Trinity Reformed Church. Brownson, his mentor, preached Tim's ordination sermon from Isaiah 50:4: "The Lord God has given me the tongue of a teacher, that I may know how to sustain the weary with a word. Morning by morning he wakens—wakens my ear to listen as those who are taught." This sermon was to set the trajectory of Tim's life and ministry. He was charged now to have the tongue of a teacher and sustain the weary with a word!

Tim entered into ordained ministry and served three churches while a pastor in the RCA. His first was Fellowship Reformed Church of Hudsonville, Michigan, where he served from 1976 to 1980. His second call was at First Reformed Church of South Holland, Illinois, where he co-pastored with his best friend, the Rev. Dave Bast, from 1980 to 1983. And his final church was Christ Memorial Church of Holland, Michigan, where he served from 1983 to 1995. During each call, Tim gave himself over to a life of Word and sacrament in which he preached, catechized, discipled, and encouraged the people he was charged to care for. During this time, Tim completed a ThM at Calvin Theological Seminary in 1981 and finished his DMin at WTS in 1992.

This was also the season in which Tim and Nancy grew a family. Tim and Nancy were blessed with three children—Sarah (b. 1974), Jon (b. 1976) and Rebekah (b. 1978). Though Tim was a dedicated pastor, he worked hard to also be present as a father and husband. This was not easy, with the requests and demands of ministry pulling his attention in multiple directions. Tim loved being a father, and he was a passionate advocate for his kids, from school plays to athletic contests to homework. He and Nancy created a home in which family was a priority.

It is impossible to talk about Tim and not talk about his wife Nancy. She was his equal partner in life and witness. Her presence created a large circumference of grace in the ministry they shared together, and its reach is impossible to measure. In their shared ministry and life, Nancy was grace without edges, always loving and long-suffering to those she interacted with. Her soft touch with congregations, students, faculty, and donors was a consequence of her deep faith and the missional conviction at the heart of their shared ministry.

Early in his life as a pastor, Tim had an experience that shaped the future of his preaching ministry. In 1979, he went with some friends to hear the actor Michael Toledo "perform" the Gospel of Mark. Toledo had memorized the entire gospel narrative, and he performed it for a paying public audience. Tim thought to himself, "If this man is willing to do memorize the gospel as an actor, why I am not doing this as a pastor?" So Tim set himself to begin internalizing every scriptural text he preached, as well as the sermon scripts he wrote. He began preaching with great effect, and while he was at Christ Memorial Church, it became one of the fastest-growing churches in the country. Tim's preaching was a homiletic cocktail, in equal parts pastorally sensitive, biblically precise, and theologically deep.

In 1994, Tim Brown, still pastor of Christ Memorial Church, received a phone call from the newly installed president of WTS, Dr. Dennis Voskuil. "Tim," said Voskuil, "I need you to hear the call of God to become the professor of preaching at WTS." Tim loved being a pastor and a preacher. It was his life's work. He was leading a flourishing congregation was well-established in his role, but in that moment, Tim heard God's call to a new vocation—the teaching of preaching. He said yes. So in the fall of 1995, Tim began his tenure as the Henry Bast Professor of Preaching at WTS.

In order to help offset his salary reduction from leaving Christ Memorial—as he was working to put three of his kids through college—Tim also agreed to be the primary admissions recruiter for the seminary. Wherever Tim was invited to preach, he kept his eye out for those whom God might be calling into ministry. Tim was invited to preach at a lot of places, so he talked to a lot of people. He would visit churches, college campus, and student ministries like InterVarsity, Young Life, and Campus Crusade for Christ, always with an eye out for young woman and men to recruit for WTS.

Tim spent over thirteen years lecturing and mentoring a generation of aspiring preachers. But while Tim taught preaching, he never stopped practicing the craft himself. He was the exception to the rule that "those who can't, teach." He was a teacher who *could.* As a professor of preaching, Tim was also on active call as an itinerant preacher for the church, traveling across the country to churches large and small, urban and rural, to preach the gospel of Jesus Christ. In 2006, he became a General Synod professor of theology for the RCA. Tim served as a professor of preaching until 2008, when, upon Voskuil's return to the classroom—his first and deepest love—Tim was unanimously appointed by the board of trustees as WTS's eleventh president.

During his tenure as president of WTS, Tim transformed both the face of the faculty as well as the physical face of the seminary. He hired fifteen new faculty and was responsible for raising a historic amount of gifts to build a new learning commons, re-imagining the library space with an eye towards the future of theological education. Tim Brown retired as the president of WTS in 2019, having been both a transformational presence in Western's history and one of the most celebrated and honored preachers in the RCA.

This book of essays honors the legacy of Tim Brown, who, in and out of season, always had the *tongue of a teacher* and *sustained the weary with a word.*

Introduction: "Come with Me"

Trygve D. Johnson

If there is a signature that captures a sermon from the Rev. Dr. Tim Brown, it is "Come with me." Tim employed this invitation before he launched into a personal story. "Come with me" was Tim's invitation to the congregation to follow a narrative trail and in the process unlock their imaginations and see what God was doing in their lives and neighborhoods. When you heard the phrase "Come with me," you found yourself leaning in, filled with an eagerness to follow and experience where this narrative might lead. Often, those of us who listened were launched into a new geography of a God-sized world from which we could never return the same.

So as an introduction to this volume of essays in honor of Tim Brown, I want to briefly tell my story with him. So, if you will, "Come with me."

It's October 1993, in Christ Chapel on the campus of Northwestern College in Orange City, Iowa. I'm a sophomore, studying history and trying to discern my future. I'm sitting in the balcony of the western choir loft, which looks down on the chapel stage. This was a routine day in the life at Northwestern College, where mandatory chapel helped us mark time, and I had few expectations going into the morning.

We welcomed Tim Brown, the senior pastor of Christ Memorial Church in Holland, Michigan, as our guest preacher. Tim stepped to the center of the chapel stage. There was no pulpit or podium. It was just him, wearing a grey suit. He had what you might call "presence." There was an open Bible in his left hand. I remember him looking around the chapel and smiling, his eyes focused on us. The chapel was still.

Tim began to speak, reciting Scripture from his heart. Like the best music pressed into vinyl, he had grooved holy Scripture into his heart and mind, proclaiming the Word with an uncommon freedom. This was an introduction to me. It was an invitation to hear Scripture spoken from the heart, with a warmth and intimacy that drew me closer to God, rather than a cool reading that made God feel distant.

Tim's sermon that morning was as precise as a surgeon with a scalpel. His eyes never looked down. There were no sermon notes. It was inside of him. In Tim's hands, the sermon was alive, as he breathed into chapel a fresh world where Christ's reign was breaking in upon us right now, a world I had always sensed was there but didn't know how to enter. Tim said, "Come with me." And I did. This invitation was like a key that unlocked me from my tame cul-de-sac and launched me into the wide-open country of salvation, where still there exists a wildness of the Spirit.

It was not just what Tim said, but how he said it. His sermon moved like a river: the narrative began wide, with a calm cadence, and then suddenly there was a bend in the course, and the currents of the sermon drew fast, narrowing its focus on Christ as the prose tightened in energy, and suddenly it felt like I was shooting through tight rapids, exhilarated, breathless, holding on for dear life. His sermon was not so much a means to communicate information as it was an experience that showed me larger vision of reality.

I sat spell-bound, riveted to my pew, as I listened to Tim expound the gospel. Something inside of me was stirring. There was a fire in my imagination. Tim's sermon unlocked a hope that I had been harboring but dared not speak aloud. It was the hope that preaching could be a vocation worthy of one's life. This man's speech revealed to me and embodied for me a quality of preaching I had been longing to hear my whole life. "*This*," I said to myself, "*this* is what preaching is supposed to be!" That morning, a preacher shattered my preconceived conceptions of what a sermon could do. Tim preached the gospel like a jazz musician improvising on a theme: the melody was loose and intuitive, yet held together as softly as breath, and it made me want to pick up an instrument, join the band, and play with him.

This was a significant gift to me. At this time in my life, I had a deep sense that I was being called to pastoral ministry, and specifically to be a preacher, but I had my doubts.

When the sermon was finished, it felt like the air was charged, the world larger, because I was placed inside the storied adventure of the gospel. After the sermon, I made my way downstairs to the main sanctuary. I asked our chaplain if he would introduce me to our guest and if I could have a conversation with him. The next day, I was invited to dinner with Tim for a conversation. Though I didn't know it at the time, this began a new relationship that would alter the trajectory of my life.

A year later, Tim would leave his pulpit at Christ Memorial, one of the fastest-growing churches in the country, to be a professor of preaching at Western Theological Seminary (WTS). At the time, the student body had been reduced to a handful of aspiring pastors. They needed to attract new students if they were going to survive. As part of his calling, Tim was tasked with going out to identify and recruit a new generation of pastors and preachers.

As part of this work, Tim recruited me to come and study with him at WTS. I was interested, but I wavered, since I was committed in my heart to a seminary closer to home in the Pacific Northwest. But over time, I felt the undeniable pull to study at WTS.

It was late summer, weeks before the fall semester was to begin. I called Tim at his house, confessed my reconsideration, and wondered if there was any way I could still enroll as a student that fall. He asked if I could give him a day. So the following day I called Tim back, and Tim said, "If you are serious about coming this fall, WTS has a place for you." He also said he had secured me a scholarship, a place to live, and an internship with Hope College Campus Ministries. I was overwhelmed. Outside my family, I had never had anyone do so much for me. This is what Tim did all the time for people. He was an advocate. I was blessed to be one of the many.

All of this was great. But I was still hoping for something more essential. On that phone call, I asked a question that would change the nature of our relationship: "Tim, if I come, will you pour your heart into me?" There was a long pause. Tim answered, "I promise." "I'm coming," I said.

There are moments in a person's life that are defining. This was one of mine. The defining moment pivoted around a promise from Tim Brown. Over the next three years from 1996 to 1999, Tim kept his promise. He poured his heart into me. He taught me in and out of the classroom, with lectures, books, conversations, and practical experiences. He invited me into his home, fed me at his table, and took me on preaching trips where we talked about ministry and life. Tim gave me his time. I learned what it looked like to be a pastor from Tim Brown, because he showed me what a pastor does. He mentored not by telling me what to do, but by showing me.

Other Stories

My story is but a drop in the bucket of how Tim's generosity in friendship and pastoral encouragement has shaped the pastoral or personal faith of many. This collection includes personal reflections and scholarly contributions from others who have their own stories of how Tim's ministry influenced or encouraged their own lives, scholarship, ministries, and friendships. There are hundreds of people who could have contributed to this book, and the essays included here represent just a few of the friends and colleagues whose lives were enriched through Tim's ministry and leadership. It is a collection created to honor the diversity and range of people Tim mentored, led, and influenced in his pastoral, professional, and presidential vocation.

One of Tim's oldest and closest friends is **David Bast**, former president of Words of Hope. His essay "What Is Preaching For?" kicks off our collection and reflects on the purpose and work of preaching. He asks the question of why we preach at all. Since their earliest days, David and Tim were bonded in friendship and vocation through an enthusiasm for Scripture and for preaching the gospel.

Jeffrey Munroe is the editor of *Reformed Journal* and author of the book *Reading Buechner*. From 2012 to 2020, he served as a vice president at Western Theological Seminary, working closely with Tim Brown during his presidency. Jeff's essay "Truth to Tell: The Influence of Frederick Buechner on Timothy Brown" pivots off the wisdom of Frederick Buechner's writing and shares how his work of the "strangeification" of language and the importance of speaking honestly was represented in Tim's preaching and leadership.

Karen Bohm Barker is emeritus professor of theatre at Northwestern College in Orange City, Iowa. Karen led worship alongside Tim at various RCA events and services, served on Western

Seminary's board of trustees during Tim's tenure as president, and team-taught a seminary course on preaching with him. Karen's essay "Descendant of Bezalel" explores a tension between Christians and the arts, as well as how she found not only a supporter and encourager in Tim Brown but also a friend.

Fred L. Johnson III is a professor of history at Hope College and has taught there since the fall of 2000. Fred's essay "More Than Just My Brother from Another Mother," is a reflection on his first meeting with Tim. Fred explores how despite differences of race and background experiences, Tim wanted to be a genuine friend and brother.

Han-luen Kantzer Komline is associate professor of church history and theology at Western Theological Seminary. She joined WTS's faculty in 2014. Han-luen's essay "Monica and Macrina: Students of Scripture, Teachers of Teachers" is a scholarly homage to Tim's support and encouragement of women in ministry and a reflection on her and Tim's binding love of Augustine.

Gail Merrick Ebersole is a retired leader of forty-three years of para-church ministry. Thirty-two of these years were spent with Young Life, where she held various roles, from area director to the first woman senior vice president. She also served ten years with InterVarsity Christian Fellowship as a vice president, overseeing their work in the south-central and later eastern U.S. Gail has served on the WTS board for eight years and is now serving as the chair of the board. Gail's essay "Woman Called by God" is a reflection on her own journey and the challenges of serving as a woman in Christian ministry, as well as how she found a friend in Tim Brown.

Trygve Johnson is the Hinga-Boersma Dean of the Chapel at Hope College. He is a former student of Tim Brown, and his essay "The Project" reflects on the homiletic instincts that he learned from Tim and continues to put into practice in his own preaching.

J. Todd Billings is the Gordon H. Girod Research Professor of Reformed Theology at Western Theological Seminary. When Todd joined the faculty at WTS in 2005, Tim Brown was a colleague who also became a friend and a "spiritual father," as he prayed with him nearly every time they would meet. Todd's essay "God's Powerful Instrument: The Triune God's Action Through Scripture" is a scholarly reflection of the power of Scripture for the Christian life, honoring his and Tim's shared commitment to the Word.

Kristen Deede Johnson is dean and vice president of academic affairs at Western Theological Seminary. Kristen's teaching and scholarship engages areas of theology, discipleship and formation, justice, culture, and political theory. She joined the WTS faculty while Tim was president. Her essay "The Jesus Way in Divided Times" is written in honor of Tim's long-lasting commitment to discipleship in theological education.

This collection of essays would not be complete without a contribution by Jon Brown. Jon is the lead pastor of Pillar Church in Holland, Michigan. He is also Tim's only son. Jon grew up witnessing the workaday life of Tim as a pastor and a preacher. He experienced first-hand the stresses and joys, the opportunities and challenges of pastoral ministry and its blessing and burden on a family. His essay "Pastor, Preacher, Parent: But the greatest of these is..." reflects on the challenges of being a parent in ministry, first and foremost being committed to be an authentic "person" to our kids. As Tim's son, it is all too appropriate that Jon have the last word!

Conclusion

Tim Brown had a long and lasting impact on those he served as a pastor, the students he taught, and the institution he led. He impacted and touched countless lives. To be sure, Tim was a preacher to be admired, but he also was a wise professor, mentor, coach, and counselor, and most importantly, he was able to graciously transition all of those roles into a friendship that sustained "the weary with a word." What is often missed when talking about Tim Brown is that his greatest gift to the church was not his preaching; it was his capacity for love and friendship. For that gift of friendship to so many, this book is dedicated in his honor.

CHAPTER 1

What Is Preaching For?

David Bast

What function is so noble, as to be
Ambassador to God, and destiny?
To open life, to give kingdoms to more
Than kings give dignities; to keep heaven's door?
Mary's prerogative was to bear Christ, so
'Tis preachers' to convey him.

—John Donne, "To Mr. Tilman After He Had Taken Orders"

I am grateful for the opportunity to contribute to this volume in honor of Tim Brown, a fellow preacher, a onetime co-pastor with me at the First Reformed Church of South Holland, Illinois, and a friend who has stuck closer than a brother since we first met in the fall of 1969 as eighteen-year-old freshmen at Hope College. Tim has gone on from there to become a beloved pastor, an influential teacher of preaching, and a transformative seminary president. But I think he most would want to be acknowledged simply as a preacher of the gospel, a "steward of God's mysteries" (1 Corinthians 4:1). So in this essay, I want to talk about preaching—specifically, its purpose or goal.

What is preaching for? What is it supposed to do? As an act of worship, the sermon functions like every other part of the service: it is meant to draw us to Christ by the power of the Spirit and through the Son to the Father. As a means of grace, preaching convicts, converts, and saves.

But more specific things can be said about the goals of preaching. Charles Simeon, the early-nineteenth-century Cambridge vicar and fellow of King's College, said that the three principal aims or ends of preaching were to instruct, to please, and to affect:

> to instruct, solve difficulties, unfold mysteries, penetrate into the ways of divine wisdom, establish truth, refute error, comfort, correct, and censure, fill the hearers with an admiration of the wonderful works and ways of God, inflame their souls with zeal, powerfully incline them to piety and holiness.[1]

Simeon was quoting there from the seventeenth-century Huguenot preacher Jean Claude, whose "Essay on the Composition of a Sermon" was hugely influential in shaping Simeon's own view and practice of preaching.[2] Simeon came to be known as the father of Anglican evangelicalism because of the impact of his vibrant personal faith and evangelical preaching upon generations of Cambridge students. He eventually published a widely distributed multi-volume set of expository sermon outlines, to which he appended an English version of Claude's essay. Channeled through Charles Simeon, Jean Claude's expository style of preaching became the ideal of English-speaking evangelicals.

It's worth expanding upon these three ends of preaching, beginning with its aim to please by filling its hearers "with an admiration of the wonderful works and ways of God." The art of oratory was highly prized in the Roman world. Facility in persuasive speech was an indispensable asset for the career-minded young Roman man. After the Constantinian establishment of Christianity, churches became the place to go to see and hear rhetoric at its best. In fact, congregations were crowded with people who would come for the sermon and then

1 Charles Simeon, *Let Wisdom Judge*, ed. Arthur Pollard (London: InterVarsity Press, 1959), 21.

2 Hugh Evan Hopkins, *Charles Simeon of Cambridge* (London: Hodder and Stoughton, 1977), 58. For Jean Claude and his "Essay on the Composition of a Sermon," see Karin Maag, "Pulpit and Pen: Pastors and Professors as Shapers of the Huguenot Tradition," in *Companion to the Huguenots*, ed. Raymond A. Mentzer and Bertrand Van Ruymbeke (Leiden: Brill, 2016), 150.

leave before the sacrament. Popular preachers were rewarded with applause—something that seems to happen nowadays in worship only to singers—and acclaimed with the waving of handkerchiefs and cries of "thirteenth apostle!" (Tim and I have often thought that a laudable custom and have used this cheer to encourage one another.)

Not surprisingly, churches still tend to want pastors who are good preachers. And what preacher doesn't want to be good? We all look out at the congregation with apprehension, lest there be nodding heads or glazed looks or, worse still, empty pews. When I was still a practicing preacher, I read an anecdote in *Leadership* magazine that perfectly captures how eager we can be to please. The story concerns George Canning, a nineteenth-century British statesman and sometime prime minister. One Sunday, Canning went to church and the vicar, excited at having so distinguished a personage in the congregation, could not resist fishing for a compliment as he shook hands at the door following the service. The exchange went like this:

> Vicar: "Mr. Canning, how did you like the sermon?"
> Canning: "Sir, you were brief."
> Vicar: "That is good; I do not like to be tedious."
> Canning: "Sir, you were also tedious."

Well, no one wants to be tedious. But perhaps some tedium in a sermon may be excused if the main purpose of preaching is actually instruction. That's an attractive idea, especially in Reformed churches with a tradition of catechetical or doctrinal preaching. Anyone who has read a seventeenth-century Puritan sermon can't help but be impressed by the mental capacity and physical stamina demanded of the congregation to whom it was delivered. Puritan sermons can come across like the treatises of systematic theology that many of them were.

But the hearing of the gospel is an encounter with grace, and this is not fundamentally an intellectual experience. That is not to say that preaching shouldn't or doesn't teach. You certainly hope to learn at least something from a sermon—at least I do. But a sermon is not a lecture, and listening to it is not a classroom exercise. What matters is not so much whether you can remember the outline or content of a sermon when it's over; what matters is what happens to you and in you while you are listening to it.

If that is the case, many would agree that what preaching really aims at is the hearers' behavioral change or moral improvement. Its purpose is to "inflame their souls with zeal" and "powerfully incline them to piety and holiness"; in other words, to change lives. The question is, how is this to be done? And the answer is not by simply issuing commands or instructions. Preachers' overuse of the imperative mood is what gave rise to the exasperated complaint "Don't preach at me!"—a retort often directed against over-solicitous attempts at personal correction. Most of the people who never actually go to church or listen to sermons tend to assume that preaching means scolding; they view the sermon as a harangue. But preaching isn't, or shouldn't be, just telling people what they ought to do and trying to guilt them into doing it.

There is a point here that must not be missed. The gospel *is* meant to change us; Calvin himself agreed. I used to have a copy of a woodcut print on my office wall with a picture of Calvin and this quote: "The word of God was not given to render us eloquent or subtle, but for the transformation of our lives." Preaching does indeed transform lives. In 1992, I was invited to preach at a special service in a little village in a rural West Bengal, India. A number of people in this village had become Christians and had formed a small congregation. These new believers were told that the radio programs that were bringing them the gospel and teaching them the Bible came from Words of Hope and the Reformed Church in America (RCA). They had no idea what the RCA was. Still, they felt like they should honor these broadcasts by using the word "reformed" in the name of their new church, so they decided to call it "The Church of the Reformed Lives." Calvin would have approved.

While acknowledging the moral effects of preaching and the fact that it should lead to reformed lives (and to reformed societies as well), it is crucial to understand that the transformation preaching seeks is produced in a unique and unexpected way. Preaching does not transform its hearers by telling them what they ought to do or not do. It is not mere exhortation, let alone harangue. Preaching changes lives by means of what the apostle called "the message of the cross." J. Gresham Machen wrote a moving statement of this truth almost a century ago:

> The early Christians, to the astonishment of their neighbors, lived a strange new kind of life—a life of honesty, of purity, and of unselfishness. And from the Christian community all other types of life were excluded in the strictest way.... But how was the life produced? It might conceivably have been produced by exhortation. That method had often been tried in the ancient world; in the Hellenistic age there were many wandering preachers

> who told men how they ought to live. But such exhortation proved to be powerless.... The strange thing about Christianity was that it...transformed lives...not by appealing to the human will, but by telling a story; not by exhortation, but by the narration of an event.... Could anything be more impractical than the attempt to influence conduct by rehearsing events concerning the death of a religious leader? ...But the strange thing is that it works.... Where the most eloquent exhortation fails, the simple story of an event succeeds; the lives of men are transformed by a piece of news.[3]

In other words, gospel preaching can do many things. Certainly it can please, move, teach, even transform. But in order to do any of those things, it must do something else first. It must tell the story, so that those who hear will come to believe it.

Faith Comes by Hearing

Before going any further in talking about the purpose of preaching, let me just say that I mean preaching *under the operation of the Holy Spirit.* This is only the word that goes out from God's mouth that, like the rain and snow sent from heaven, accomplishes the purpose for which he sends it. The apostle noted that the treasure of the gospel is entrusted to the clay jars of our fallible human natures "so that it may be made clear that this extraordinary power belongs to God and does not come from us" (2 Corinthians 4:7).

Furthermore, if as preachers we can do nothing of eternal consequence apart from the Spirit's work, the same is true of our hearers. All public speakers are encouraged to know their audience. Basing our analysis on Scripture, we can identify three basic facts about the natural spiritual state of the people we preach to. One, they are blind; two, they are hard; three, they are dead. Unbelievers are blind to the identity and significance of Christ: "the god of this world has blinded the minds of the unbelievers, to keep them from seeing the light of the gospel of the glory of Christ, who is the image of God" (2 Corinthians 4:4). Far from being open to the life of God, they in fact are ignorant of it and unreceptive to it: "They are darkened in their understanding, alienated from the life of God because of the ignorance that is in them, due to their hardness of heart" (Ephesians 4:18). And finally, in spiritual terms they are dead: "You were dead through the

3 J. Gresham Machen, *Christianity and Liberalism* (New York, MacMillan, 1923), 47ff.

trespasses and sins in which you once lived, following the course of this world" (Ephesians 2:1-2a). Clearly, then, human language—even persuasive or eloquent language—can't do much to change that. Something supernatural is demanded.

But the Word of God in the power of the Spirit can raise the spiritually dead. "Very truly, I tell you, the hour is coming, *and is now here*, when the dead will hear the voice of the Son of God, and those who hear will live" (John 5:25, emphasis mine). I was visiting once with a pastor who broadcasted messages in the Hmong language to tribal people living in the highlands of Vietnam and Laos. He showed me a packet his listeners had recently mailed him. It contained many pages of names—hundreds of them. With it came a cover letter that said, "Dear Pastor John, we heard you speaking on the radio about the Lamb's book of life, and we would like you please to enter our names in that book." How do you explain something like that? Only the way Jesus did. He "calls his own sheep by name and leads them out...and the sheep follow him because they know his voice" (John 10:3-4). This is what gives confidence to preaching. If we speak of the Lord from the Word, we know that the Spirit will cause some to recognize his voice and begin to follow him.

So yes, unless the Lord uses the sermon, those who preach it labor in vain and those who hear it listen in vain. But we all still have to do something, both those who preach and those who hear.

Back, then, to the initial question: what is preaching for? What is it actually supposed to do? What is it meant to accomplish? It is meant to produce saving faith in Christ. This is the point of the very first Christian sermon, preached by Peter on the day of Pentecost. Boiled down to essentials, Peter's sermon went like this: "This is Jesus. You killed him, God raised him, and we are witnesses." When the crowd that heard him was cut to the heart and asked what they should do, Peter replied,

> "Repent, and be baptized every one of you in the name of Jesus Christ so that your sins may be forgiven." ...So those who welcomed his message were baptized. (Acts 2:37, 41)

That producing faith in Christ is the primary purpose of preaching is also a key part of Paul's explanation of the mechanics of salvation in Romans 10. It's not that hard to be saved, says the apostle. You don't have to establish your own righteousness through the law. You don't have to climb up to heaven or descend to the abyss to find a savior. All you have to do is call on the name of the Lord. Of course, this "calling" isn't some sort of magic incantation. It is the prayer of faith. The name of the Lord is "Jesus." And the faith that calls on his name for salvation comprises both an inward conviction about the truth of the gospel and an outward confession of the Lord Jesus,

> because if you confess with your lips that Jesus is Lord and believe in your heart that God raised him from the dead, you will be saved. For one believes with the heart and so is justified, and one confesses with the mouth and so is saved. (Romans 10:9-10)

How do people get to the point where they have both the knowledge and the faith to call on Jesus in this way? This is where preaching comes in:

> But how are they to call on one in whom they have not believed? And how are they to believe in one of whom they have never heard? And how are they to hear without someone to proclaim him? And how are they to proclaim him unless they are sent?
>
> ...So faith comes from what is heard, and what is heard comes through the word of Christ. (Romans 10:14-17)

What is not always noted in this passage, though, is the specific point Paul is making. That comes in verse 16, which is often omitted (because it's awkward) when quoting from Romans 10: "But not all have obeyed the good news; for Isaiah says, 'Lord, who has believed our message?'" Paul is wrestling in this section of Romans with the heartbreaking tragedy of the rejection of the gospel by the majority of the Jewish people. The problem isn't with the gospel message; that's clear. The problem isn't that they haven't heard the gospel; preachers have been sent, and the message has been heard, and the name of Jesus has been made known. The problem is the failure of some hearers to "obey the gospel"; that is, to respond to the good news about Jesus with repentance and faith and call upon his name for salvation. The breakdown isn't in the preaching, it's in the believing; so it's not on us, the apostle is saying, it's on them.

I wonder if we can be as sure that our preaching is not to blame for people's failure to respond to the gospel. There is a tacit, and often quite open, assumption of universal salvation among many preachers and churches today. The liberal church has long embraced some sort of universalism, but now many evangelicals are doing so as well—generally by promoting the idea that all things and all people will somehow be included in Christ's redeeming work. It's as though they read Romans 1:16-17 and affirm that the gospel is the power of God for salvation for the Jew first and also for the Greek—whether people believe it or not, whether they turn to Christ in faith or reject him in contempt. There are statements in the New Testament of breathtaking scope. So yes, we rejoice in the promise that God will reconcile all things to himself through Christ (Colossians 1:20). In humility and charity, we refrain from speculating about the fate of any individual, whether believer or unbeliever; it's not ours to judge. We praise the unfathomable mercy of the God who wills all to be saved and wishes that none might perish (1 Timothy 2:4, 2 Peter 3:9). And we leave all final questions of salvation with him.

But none of this means we can ignore the overwhelming emphasis in the New Testament on the need to repent, believe the gospel, and publicly confess faith in Christ. Why else did Peter urge the Pentecost converts to be baptized? When the Philippian jailer cried out, "What must I do to be saved?" Paul didn't reply, "Nothing. God loves you just the way you are. Have a nice day!" We must not preach—or listen—as if a person's response to the gospel doesn't really matter, as if the good news of Christ's death and resurrection is a take-it-or-leave-it proposition. To those who refuse to accept it, the gospel doesn't mean power for salvation; it doesn't mean anything at all. In fact, it means less than nothing. For such people, the message of the cross is an object of ridicule or cause of offense:

> For the message about the cross is foolishness to those who are perishing.... For Jews demand signs and Greeks desire wisdom, but we proclaim Christ crucified, a stumbling block to Jews and foolishness to Gentiles. (1 Corinthians 1:18, 22)

Moreover, we should face squarely the implications of the view that faith in Christ is optional, like a luxury accessory on a new car—nice to have, but not absolutely necessary. If it isn't true that everyone must call upon the name of the Lord Jesus to be saved, then we do no favors to people when we preach the gospel to them, because confessing and following Christ Jesus as Lord is hard. And it's particularly hard in cultures where the traditional religion is hostile to Christianity. If it's all the same whether they believe or not, then we had better leave people alone in their unbelief. B. B. Warfield offered some blunt words for those who consider Christian faith to be nonessential for salvation. If all religions are equal ways to God, then

> The whole missionary work of the church is an impertinence, the whole history of the church a gigantic error; the great commission itself a crime against humanity—launching the Christian world upon a fool's errand, every step of which has dripped with wasted blood. Surely the proclamation of the gospel is made, then, mere folly, and the blood of the martyrs becomes only the measure of the narrow fanaticism of earlier and less enlightened times.[4]

This is a high responsibility for all preachers who would be faithful to the apostolic teaching of the New Testament and the historic evangelical mission of the church. We must believe and preach Christ as Savior and Lord. The apostle speaks for himself and for all faithful preachers: "We do not proclaim ourselves; we proclaim Jesus Christ as Lord" (2 Corinthians 4:5). "Jesus is Lord" is an absolute claim. If it's true, then Jesus is Lord of everyone everywhere, and everyone needs to know that and respond to him in faith. If it isn't true, then we have no business preaching at all.

The preaching of the gospel is not merely a matter of proclamation but of invitation as well. Preachers who actually believe the gospel must also call on everyone to respond to it in faith. So, like Paul in Caesarea, we must follow gospel proclamation with an evangelical appeal: "King Agrippa, do you believe the prophets? I know that you believe" (Acts 26:27).

Early in his career as a reformer, Luther described the primary purpose of preaching with characteristic clarity and vigor:

> "It is not enough to preach the works, life and words of Christ as historical facts, as if the knowledge of these would suffice for the conduct of life.... Rather ought Christ to be preached to the end that faith in him may be established—that he may not only be Christ, but be Christ for you and me, that what is said of him and is denoted in his name may be effectual in us. Such faith is produced and preserved in us by preaching why Christ came, what he brought and bestowed, what benefit it is to us to accept him."[5]

Jesus is both Lord and Christ; nothing can change that. But the reason to preach for faith is that he may be Christ for you and me.

4 B. B. Warfield, "False Religions and the True," in *The Power of God unto Salvation* (Presbyterian Board of Publication and Sabbath-School Work, 1903).

5 Martin Luther, "The Freedom of a Christian," in *Three Treatises* (Philadelphia, Fortress Press, 1970), 292ff.

There's one more thing to say about preaching and faith, something I've learned from personal experience. Preaching doesn't just lead to an initial faith in Christ; it continues to renew and sustain it: "those who prophesy speak to other people for their upbuilding and encouragement and consolation" (1 Corinthians 14:3). In Luther's words, faith is both produced and preserved by the preaching of Christ. My faith is susceptible to the corrosive effects of the world, the flesh, and the devil. Doubts can undermine it, stubborn sins or unanswered prayers seem to mock it, sorrows cast it into shadow. In *The Pilgrim's Progress*, one of the scenes Christian is shown in the House of the Interpreter is a fire burning against a wall. An evil one is continually casting water upon it to quench it. But the fire still burns higher and hotter because Christ is on the other side of the wall, pouring on the oil of grace. The oil that replenishes my faith and rekindles my devotion most often comes to me through the reading and hearing of the word of God—and not infrequently through a sermon while I myself am preaching it. I have often felt the thrill of new assurance and greater love for Christ as I proclaimed him from the Scriptures. This is why I object to the phrase "You're preaching to the choir," as if that's wasted and unnecessary effort. The choir needs preaching too. In fact, never mind the choir. Preachers need preaching, perhaps more than most.

A number of years ago, I was invited to join the board of an independent mission organization. At my first meeting I was invited to share my testimony with the other members of the board and staff. It went something like this: "I was born and raised in a devout Christian home. From infancy I was exposed to the faithful preaching of the gospel. I can't remember a time when I did not love the Lord Jesus and trust him as my Savior. So I can't tell you the first time I was converted. But the last time was a couple of days ago." A lot of Baptist heads nodded around the table. Conversion is not a one-and-done deal. Repentance is a daily, lifelong exercise of faith, of turning again and again from self and sin and folly to embrace Jesus. Preaching calls us to do that—and actually causes it to happen.

William Tyndale meant these words as counsel for Bible readers, but they make equally good advice for Bible preachers:

> The scripture is that wherewith God draweth us unto him. The scriptures sprang out of God, and flow unto Christ, and were given to lead us to Christ. Thou must therefore go along by the

> scripture as by a line, until thou comest at Christ, which is the way's end and resting place.[6]

So let us preach Christ. Let us preach from faith, to faith, and for faith—our own as well as others'. Whatever part of the Bible we may be preaching, let us follow it until we reach Christ, who is both the way and the end. Let us preach Christ with such power and conviction that all who believe become part of the church of reformed lives. Because that's what preaching is for.

I began with a poem; let me end with a prayer:

> O Lord, ...give testimony to the Word preached, and glorify it in the hearts of all who hear; may it enlighten the ignorant, awaken the careless, reclaim the wandering, establish the weak, comfort the fearful, make ready a people for their Lord.[7]

6 William Tyndale, qtd. in P. E. Hughes, *The Theology of the English Reformers* (Grand Rapids, MI: Eerdmans, 1965), 58.

7 *The Valley of Vision: A Collection of Puritan Prayers and Devotions*, ed. Arthur Bennet (Edinburgh: Banner of Truth, 1975), 379.

CHAPTER 2

Truth to Tell: The Influence of Frederick Buechner on Timothy Brown

Jeffrey Munroe

Introduction

In 1992, the author-minister Frederick Buechner spoke at Calvin College. I failed to anticipate the size of the crowd he would attract that night and arrived about twenty minutes early to find the auditorium doors closed because the venue was full. I wasn't the only one to underestimate the crowd—upon arriving on campus and seeing all the parked cars, Buechner asked his host if there were a sporting event or concert going on that would account for the overflowing parking lots.

My timing proved serendipitous. A plan had been hastily devised to handle the crowd, and folding chairs were set up on the stage a few feet away from where Buechner would stand. I was shown to one of those prize seats. My unexpected fortune had another benefit as well. I could glance over my shoulder and scan the crowd for familiar faces. I saw Tim Brown almost immediately, in the middle of the auditorium, along with the ministry staff of Christ Memorial Church.

I was impressed.

It wasn't just Tim's ability to anticipate crowd size that impressed me. I was impressed that Tim Brown was there at all. At that time, Christ Memorial was one of the fastest-growing churches in the country. When you're a megachurch pastor like Tim, you don't necessarily attend events as a participant—you headline them. Yes, the crowd Frederick Buechner drew to Calvin College that night was impressive, but a larger crowd would gather at Christ Memorial the next Sunday morning to hear Tim preach. Later, I would learn that the Christ Memorial team was on a day-long retreat, and that afternoon Tim had shown them the Richard Dreyfuss and Bill Murray movie *What About Bob?* They'd discussed it as a ministry parable before going to hear Buechner. Imagine: Bob Wiley and Frederick Buechner on the same day!

What drew Tim Brown to Frederick Buechner?

Some thirty years later, I would join Tim's team at Western Theological Seminary (WTS). By that time, Tim had left Christ Memorial to become professor of preaching at Western, and a few years before I arrived, Tim had been named president of the seminary. When I joined the team, we met every Wednesday morning in Tim's spacious office. There were two distinct areas in that L-shaped room. At one end was his desk, but in the other part there was a conference table surrounded on three sides by bookshelves. I spent a lot of time at that conference table and had ample opportunity to peruse Tim's collection of books. His Buechner library was extensive. These were books Tim had picked up while at Christ Memorial. Occasionally, before our meetings started, I would take one of the Buechner volumes off the shelf and thumb through it. I found slips of paper stuck into various pages and lots of underlining. These books weren't for show; they were "working books."

On the surface, Tim Brown and Frederick Buechner have very little in common. Tim was a megachurch pastor, preaching professor, and seminary president. Although Buechner was ordained in the Presbyterian Church, he never pastored a congregation, and after a few years as a minister and English teacher at an exclusive Eastern boarding school, he spent most of his career living in rural Vermont writing novels, memoirs, and essays and dabbling in preaching. I am quite sure that if you ask Tim who his ministry hero is, he would quickly say Eugene Peterson. However, I contend that Frederick Buechner has significantly influenced Tim (and, although not my topic here, Eugene Peterson as well). In this essay, I will focus on Buechner as a preacher and consider the impact he's had on Tim Brown, particularly

Buechner's emphasis on truth-telling and ability to hold a listener's attention through what I call the "strangeification" of language.

Buechner's Sacred Journey

Frederick Buechner was born in 1926 to a family that was not involved in the life of the church. Buechner's father was plagued with alcoholism and mental illness, and although there was wealth in his extended family, he struggled mightily to make his way in the world. Buechner's childhood was marked by frequent moves as his father tried new jobs. There were dark and difficult episodes, punctuated by his father's suicide when Buechner was only ten. The family's response was hardly functional—there was no funeral, and the father was not spoken of afterward. Not only was his suicide a family secret; his very existence became a family secret.

After a brief sojourn to Bermuda, Buechner was sent to prep school at Lawrenceville in New Jersey and later attended Princeton University. At Lawrenceville, his interest and gifts with words began to emerge, and while still a student at Princeton, he began writing his first novel, *A Long Day's Dying*, which was published in January 1950. Buechner's novel was a smash hit, and he was hailed by critics and the literati as an emerging force in American letters. A second novel, *The Seasons' Difference,* followed, and it was as much a failure as the first novel had been a success. After graduation from Princeton, Buechner secured a position on the faculty at his alma mater, Lawrenceville. He left Lawrenceville following the success of *A Long Day's Dying* and moved to New York City to pursue writing full time. However, the failure of his second novel caused an existential crisis, and Buechner was adrift, trying to figure out a career direction. He considered advertising and even at one point entertained a career in the CIA.

His apartment was close to Madison Avenue Presbyterian Church, whose pulpit was graced by the great homelitician George Buttrick. For lack of anything better to do, Buechner began attending Sunday services to hear Buttrick's eloquent sermons. One Sunday morning, Buttrick was comparing the recent coronation of Queen Elizabeth II to the crown Jesus had been offered but refused when tempted by Satan in the wilderness. Buttrick then spoke of how Jesus is indeed crowned again and again in the lives of believers, "amid confession and tears and with great laughter." Something happened inside of Buechner when Buttrick said "great laughter." Buechner would compare it to Atlantis rising from the sea or the Great Wall of China collapsing. Buechner had entered the service a religious seeker and exited a nascent follower of Christ.

Not sure what to do about this unexpected turn in his life, Buechner visited Buttrick in his office a few days later. Buttrick told Buechner he could give him a few books to read to start him on his way, but Buechner instead said that he felt he should attend seminary. Buttrick resisted, saying at one point that it would be a shame to trade a fine novelist for a mediocre preacher. Buechner was insistent, and as their conversation ended, Buttrick got his hat and coat and drove Buechner north to Union Theological Seminary at the top of Manhattan, where Buechner enrolled as a student.

At Union, Buechner took classes from a remarkable faculty, including legendary figures like Reinhold Niebuhr, Paul Tillich, and Buechner's favorite, James Muilenburg. (Muilenburg grew up in the American Reformed Church in Orange City, Iowa, and in the 1960s would spend a year as a visiting faculty member at WTS.) Following his graduation in the late 1950s, Buechner was ordained in the Presbyterian Church (he would often say that ordination was the worst career move a novelist could make) and became school minister and teacher of English at Phillips Exeter Academy in New Hampshire. It was at Exeter that Buechner's preaching skills were honed. The civil unrest and explosions of the 1960s around race and the Vietnam War were beginning, and many of the all-male Exeter students identified as "negos," negative about authority figures of any kind, including the school minister who presided over their mandatory chapel services. Reflecting years later about preaching to those students, Buechner said,

> I had a strong suspicion that once they left Exeter, most of my captive listeners would never be caught dead in church again.... It might be the last time anybody would try to persuade them that religious faith was not as boring, banal, irrelevant, and outmoded as they thought it was.... I tried every way I could think of to catch their attention and make them listen. I avoided traditional religious language and imagery as much as possible as well as the kind of fuzziness, bombast, and sentimentality that preachers are apt to resort to when all else fails...I never took it for granted that they believed any of even the most basic affirmations of the

> Christian faith concerning such matters as God and Jesus, sin and salvation, but always tried to speak to their skepticism and to honor their doubts. I made a point of never urging on them anything I did not believe myself. I was candid about what, like them, I was puzzled by and uncertain of. I tried to be myself. I tried to be honest.[1]

Buechner admitted that sometimes he could see that the young people in the school chapel were listening in spite of themselves. They were drawn to his style, his way with words, and above all else his unflinching honesty. Buechner's capacity for "telling the truth" became a hallmark. When he delivered the Beecher Lectures on preaching at Yale in the mid-1970s, he named his messages "Telling the Truth."

Telling the Truth

The sort of honesty Buechner employed at Exeter can be a challenge for preachers. The temptation, according to Buechner, is for preachers to become "peddlers" of God's word who treat the gospel like slick salesmen and say whatever they think will go down easiest, "what costs them the least to tell and what will gain them the most." There is a temptation to tell stories, but not "our real stories, not stories about what lies beneath all our other problems, which is the problem of being human, the problem of trying to hold fast somehow to Christ when much of the time, both in ourselves and in our world, it is as if Christ had never existed."[2] Telling the truth about the struggles of life, the struggles between faith and doubt, may cost a great deal and not gain the preacher anything but empty stares from the congregation. Faith, according to Buechner, is difficult.

There's a telling scene in one of Buechner's novels that captures this. The con man–evangelist–saint Leo Bebb is talking to his son-in-law Antonio Parr, the narrator, about the nature of belief.

> "I'll tell you one thing about what it's all about, and that is that it's hard, Antonio. It's all of it hard. Right down to the end. Even the things are supposed to be easy, they're hard too.... You ever seen anything getting born looked easy, Antonio, let alone anything getting born again?"

1 Frederick Buechner, *Secrets in the Dark: A Life in Sermons* (San Francisco: HarperSanFrancisco, 2006), xiv.

2 Frederick Buechner, *A Room Called Remember: Uncollected Pieces* (San Francisco: Harper & Row, 1984), 48.

> From behind, Bebb had no neck to speak of, just a coil of fat above his collar. He looked diminished against the huge sky.
>
> I said, "At least it's nice you believe there's something left of Herman Redpath to sweat with."
>
> "Listen," Bebb said. "That's not even a half of what I believe."
>
> "What else do you believe?" I said.
>
> "Antonio," Bebb said, "I believe everything."
>
> It was a remark of such classic grandeur that for a few moments I sat there in the twilight silent before the sheer magnitude of it.
>
> "You make it sound almost easy," I said finally.
>
> "Don't kid yourself," Bebb said, turning slowly to where he could look at me. "It's hard as hell."[3]

Faith is hard as hell. That's not an upbeat, winning message, and as a result, many preachers are reluctant to admit how hard being a Christian can be, to admit that belief is a much more difficult path than unbelief. I recently had a conversation with someone in the Christian publishing world who spoke about discovering Buechner and being amazed because Buechner was the first Christian writer whom she'd encountered who was actually honest about the difficulty of the Christian life.

Buechner felt he couldn't be anything but honest as he spoke to those Exeter students. He imagined his listeners all having the question "Is it true?" emblazoned on their foreheads. Later, after leaving Exeter, he imagined every congregation he preached to the same way. No matter who his listeners were, he imagined an Exeter student inside each of them, asking the same question: can the story the minister is telling possibly be true?

Therefore, Buechner says that it is incumbent upon preachers to give evidence of their own wrestling with the great questions of the battle of light and dark, belief and unbelief, and sin and grace. There should be evidence that the preacher is a human being just like the rest of the congregation, evidence that the preacher has been in love, failed, worried about life and raising children and having enough money. Not that the sermon should be about those things or that the preacher should engage in some sort of narcissistic therapy session with the congregation, but that the sermon should arise *out of* those realities.

3 Frederick Buechner, *The Book of Bebb* (New York: Antheneum, 1979), 142–43.

Honesty about life should stand somehow around and under the sermon. There ought to be a sense that the preacher is talking about what matters most. As Buechner told an interviewer,

> In other words, let me speak out of my heart to your heart, let me tell you why it is that I believe, when I talk about sin, when I talk about faith, when I talk about salvation, what in my own experience I'm really talking about. A lot of people say, well, you can't make this sort of ego trip, you can't use the first person. Minsters are afraid of the first person for some reason. Maybe because they feel their own experience is so meager they don't want to display it. You don't have to use the "I" all the time to talk out of your own experience.[4]

It's an art not to preach *about* your experience but preach *out of* that experience. In the end, it's not so much the minister's story as the Bible's story that gets told. The story of the Bible is universal and applies to every listener: a story of creation, rebellion, and redemption. Buechner continues:

> We all have the same story. It's the story that the Bible tells us, for all its amorphousness, vastness, the sixty-six books. It's the plot of the Bible, the story of the Bible, that God makes the world, and the world gets lost, and for the rest of history, God is at work in the world trying somehow to bring it back to himself. That would be another way of describing the story that you and I have in common, the sense of being lost, the sense of these moments in our own lives in the depths when something is reaching out to us. And so I talk out of that.[5]

In his Beecher lectures, Buechner called the story of the Bible "Tragedy, Comedy, and Fairy Tale." It is tragedy first, bad news before it is good news. Sin is real and must be spoken of honestly. The world is broken, and our lives are broken. Terrible things happen for no apparent reason. Lazarus falls sick and Jesus does not come when summoned. So Lazarus dies. Good news happens after that, but the story of Lazarus is a bad-news story of God's absence first. Lazarus foreshadows the

4 Donald Wilson Stake, "Conversation with Frederick Buechner 'On Preaching,'" *Reformed Liturgy & Music* (Spring 1994): 59–60.

5 Stake, "Conversation," 60.

ultimate story about how Jesus, the Messiah, the savior of the world, is nailed to a cross and the world falls dark. Too often preachers give in to the temptation to skip over the bad news and get right to the good news. Telling the truth means telling the whole truth, including the sad news of sin, brokenness, suffering, and the apparent absence of God.

The gospel as comedy hearkens back to Buechner's conversion and George Buttrick's phrase "great laughter." The gospel is comedy because it is such a surprise. Ancient Abraham and Sarah are told they are going to have a baby, and Sarah can't help but laugh. In Buechner's marvelous phrase, "Only a fool would believe that a woman with one foot in the grave was soon going to have her other foot in the maternity ward."[6] Abraham and Sarah would name their baby Isaac, the Hebrew word for laughter.

Finally, the gospel is fairy tale because it is a happy-ever-after story, a story too good not to be true. Buechner doesn't mean fairy tale in the "make believe" sense, but in the sense of a story set where a battle between good and evil rages and good ultimately triumphs. The gospel story didn't just happen once upon a time, but keeps happening now and forever. The job of the preacher is to "tell the truth of the Gospel in its highest and wildest and holiest sense."[7]

In a *Christianity Today* article in 2017, Russell Moore wrote of Buechner's appeal:

> "This was someone who didn't seek to manipulate my emotions or enlist me in a cause. He just told the truth as he saw it.... Buechner does not always say what I want him to say, but I never wonder if he's telling me anything less than what he believes to be the truth. In an era of kinetic marketing and spin—as much within the church as anywhere else—that alone is remarkable."[8]

Buechner's call is for preachers to have the courage to speak honestly, to tell the truth, and in doing that move their listeners from the shallows to the depths.

6 Frederick Buechner, *Wishful Thinking: A Seeker's ABC* (San Francisco: HarperSanFrancisco, 1993), 29.

7 Frederick Buechner, *Telling the Truth: The Gospel as Tragedy, Comedy, and Fairy Tale* (New York, Harper & Row, 1990), 90.

8 Russell Moore, "How Frederick Buechner Blessed My Life," *Christianity Today*, October 2017, 46, 48.

Tell it Strange

In his book *Why Poetry,* Matthew Zapruder cites an essay by the obscure Russian writer Viktor Shklovsky called "Art as Technique." In this essay, Shklovsky attempts to explain what makes something not just an informative text but a work of art. Zapruder writes,

> According to Shklovsky, artistic texts use the exact same language as texts designed primarily to convey information, but do something different with it. The specific mechanism by which language becomes not merely a conduit to convey meaning, but something more, is called, in Russian, *ostraneniye,* most often translated as "defamiliarization," though a more literal translation would be something like "strangefying."[9]

Shklovsky says we go through life perceiving things in habitual, normal, automatic ways. We use words without thinking about them. The goal of art is to "defamiliarize," so we can experience something in a new, fresh way, echoing Abraham Joshua Heschel's famous line about actually knowing what we see instead of just seeing what we know. In Shklovsky's words:

> The purpose of art is to impart the sensation of things as they are perceived and not as they are known. The technique of art is to make objects "unfamiliar," to make forms difficult, to increase the difficulty and length of perception because the process of perception is an aesthetic end in itself and must be prolonged.[10]

Zapruder quotes Shklovsky to make the point that poetry is a form of defamiliarization and says, "Therefore, it is in poetry that we see most clearly and powerfully, without any other ultimate distraction, how language can be made deliberately strange, how it becomes especially 'a difficult, roughened, impeded language,' in order to jar us awake."[11]

Great preachers do the same thing, using ordinary language in unique ways to jar us awake. One way to do this is through adding what poets call "perception-changing modifiers," that is, by putting two words together that typically don't go together. Think of the title of the first book of Buechner's sermons from Phillips Exeter: *The Magnificent Defeat.* How in the world is defeat magnificent? The title

9 Matthew Zapruder, *Why Poetry* (New York: HarperCollins, 2017), 41–42.

10 Qtd. in Zapruder, *Why Poetry*, 42.

11 Zapruder, *Why Poetry*, 43.

of Buechner's next book of sermons, *The Hungering Dark,* contains the same sense of language strangeness. How can the dark be hungry? In other Buechner sermons he speaks of "everyman's land" instead of "no man's land," and the resurrection as a time when "all heaven broke loose." A writing teacher of mine once said that when we put together words that don't normally go together, we are creating a kind of chemical reaction between them, and the result is something new and altogether different. The trick is to use everyday language in ways it is not used every day.

Buechner's sermon "The Magnificent Defeat" is drawn from the account in Genesis 32 of Jacob wrestling a mysterious opponent all night on the banks of the Jabbok River. No one knows exactly whom Jacob wrestled. During the night, Jacob and the mysterious stranger fight to a draw, until, as the sun is rising, the stranger reaches out and touches Jacob and puts his hip out of joint. The stranger asks to be released, but Jacob won't release him without getting a blessing from the stranger first. The man then renames Jacob "Israel," saying, "you have striven with God and with humans, and have prevailed" (Genesis 32:28). Just as no one knows who Jacob's opponent was that night, no one can definitively say what the meaning of that story is. In that way, the story is inexhaustible. Buechner calls it "an ancient, jagged-edged story, dangerous and crude as a stone knife," and says, "let us not assume that it means anything very neat or very edifying."[12] As his sermon on Jacob's encounter concludes, Buechner says,

> Power, success, happiness, as the world knows them, are his who will fight for them hard enough; but peace, love, joy, are only from God. And God is the enemy whom Jacob fought there by the river, of course, and whom in one way or another we all of us fight—God, the beloved enemy. Our enemy because, before giving us everything, he demands of us everything; before giving us life, he demands our lives—our selves, our wills, our treasure.[13]

Calling God our "beloved enemy" is another example of a perception-changing modifier. Who says that? It's strange. But it's perfect.

Buechner then ends by speaking of Jacob "limping home against the great conflagration of the dawn" and draws a parallel to Jesus "staggering on broken feet out of the tomb toward the Resurrection, bearing on his body the proud insignia of the defeat which is victory,

[12] Frederick Buechner, *The Magnificent Defeat* (New York: The Seabury Press, 1966), 11.

[13] Buechner, *The Magnificent Defeat,* 18.

the magnificent defeat of the human soul at the hands of God."[14]

The "magnificent defeat," then, is three things at once. It is Jacob being wounded while wrestling the stranger at the Jabbok. It is Jesus on the cross. And it is the sublimation of the human will to God. By making language strange through a perception-changing modifier, Buechner gets our attention. Perhaps you've read that sermon before and thought "Buechner's language is poetic." But what exactly is poetic about it? It's the way the words are ordered and paired, causing a sort of chemical reaction and jarring us to attention.

Buechner spoke about the chemical reaction that comes when words are put together in new ways in his memoir *Now and Then*:

> Words—especially religious words, words that have to do with the depth of things—get tired and stale the way people do. Find new words or put old words together in combinations that make them heard as new, make you yourself new, and make you understand in new ways. "Blessed are the meek" are the words of the English translators—words of great beauty and power—but over the years they have become almost too familiar to hear any more. "*Heureux sont les debonnaires*" are the French words—Blessed are the debonair—and suddenly new beauty, new power, flood in like light. Blessed is Fred Astaire in white tie and tails. Blessed is Oliver Hardy in rusty black suit and derby hat as he picks his dapper way toward the unseen banana peel on the sidewalk.[15]

One of the things art does, according to Buechner, is get us to pay attention to life in the particular moment we encounter it: "What these works of literature or of art are doing is to say, *Stop Thinking.* Stop expecting. Stop living in the past. Stop living in the future. Stop doing anything and just pay attention to *this*."[16] Buechner related a story about paying attention that I easily relate to. The biggest town near his home in Vermont is Rutland. To get to Rutland, he would drive through a much smaller town named Wallingford. He drove that route untold times and often found himself wondering if he'd passed through Wallingford yet. It would only be by arriving at Rutland that he'd know for certain he'd been in Wallingford. "If somebody had taken a photograph of me as I was going through Wallingford, they would've

14 Buechner, *The Magnificent Defeat*, 18.

15 Frederick Buechner, *Now and Then* (New York: Harper & Row, 1993), 93.

16 Frederick Buechner, *The Remarkable Ordinary* (Grand Rapids, MI: Zondervan, 2017), 22.

taken a photograph of a human being who was not at that moment living his life. I was not present inside of my skin then, I did not see anything because I was so caught up in an inner dialogue."[17]

We all get lost in our heads, often during sermons. The "strangeification" of language is way to get people to wake up and pay attention.

Tim Brown told me once that a guest preacher had visited Christ Memorial and paid him a compliment after the service, telling Tim he was a very good preacher. "How would you know that?" Tim asked. "Because your people pay attention." Many times I've climbed into pulpits in various churches as a guest preacher and felt that I had only ten or twenty seconds to grab the congregation's attention. Sometimes the magic happens, but many times it does not. The faces glaze over, and you might as well be trying to sell them new windows or aluminum siding as share the gospel of Jesus Christ. Telling the truth "strange" is a strategy for gaining the congregation's attention.

Conclusion

It is my contention that Buechner's dedication to truth-telling and his creative use of language have had a profound influence on Timothy Brown. I have listened to Tim preach in California and Iowa, Arizona and Illinois, Florida and Colorado, and countless times in the chapel at WTS. With the possible exception of Tim's wife Nancy, I probably heard more of Tim's sermons than anyone between the years 2012 and 2019. Did I ever once doubt that Tim was telling the truth? Never. I never thought for a moment that Tim was saying anything he didn't believe.

The prevailing wisdom is that Tim's greatest gift is his prodigious ability to recite long scriptural passages from memory. I certainly admire that skill, but am not sure I agree. I believe his greatest preaching gift is his genuine faith and the passion he conveys about that faith. He never stands in a pulpit as a salesman, or, as Buechner said, "a peddler." Tim speaks honestly from the depths of his being. He tells the truth.

And he puts words together in a memorable fashion. I know a little secret about Tim. He labors over his sermons. To his listeners, who never see him use a note or manuscript, he comes across as spontaneous. That is not accurate. Before the sermon is delivered "spontaneously," there is a manuscript. And that manuscript is worked

[17] Buechner, *The Remarkable Ordinary,* 29.

on. During our travels, I'd see his manuscripts sticking out of his bag in the back seat of rental cars or lying on the table in motel rooms. The manuscript would be typed, and inevitably there would be pencil marks all over it. (Tim never leaves home without a raft of pencils in his bag.) He edits mercilessly, looking for just the right phrase, measuring the way the words sound and the chemical reactions he could create by putting words next to each other in fresh and new ways. More than once, I would think, "that's really creative," as I heard an unexpected phrase come from Tim's mouth. I knew enough not to say afterwards, "Tim, those words were strange," but they *were* strange, in all the good ways outlined above.

It was my great pleasure to serve at WTS alongside Tim in the 2010s. I congratulate him now on his retirement, and I advise new generations of preachers that they would be wise to emulate Frederick Buechner and Timothy Brown and commit themselves both to telling the truth and the creative "strangeification" of language.

CHAPTER 3

A Testimony of Belonging

Karen Bohm Barker

College Professors Need to Be Careful

My husband Jeff and I recently listened to a former student's podcast. In it, she talks about a conversation she had with Jeff while she and a few other students were on a trip with him. What Jeff said stuck with her these twenty years since her graduation and helped form her. As we listened, I looked over at him; he shook his head. No memory of the event. He simply said, "College professors need to be careful what they say."

Anyone who teaches has this happen to them. A former student credits you with something profound, something that changed them. You are grateful for the credit but have no recollection of it. When it happens to me, I'm always grateful they remember positive life-altering moments instead of the scores of times I said something ridiculous or embarrassing. Every time, what I believe about teaching is affirmed. You see, they rarely tell me they remember something life-altering about Eugene O'Neill from Dramatic Lit class or from their senior seminar research or from the Stanislavski acting method. It's invariably something I said informally or off the cuff. So while mastering my subject matter is important, so is mastering the way I think and live. My students are watching everything about me, and they are listening to the words I say that are not scripted into my lecture or lesson plan.

I find theatre to be a tangible example of the Bible's metaphor of one body with many parts. I believe that everyone embodies some kind of creativity. Because doing theatre well requires such a wide range of skills, it is an excellent place to begin to uncover one's creativity. People need to design the sets, props, costumes, posters, lights, and sound, using technical skills alongside artistic skills. People need to build props and sets, using all the mechanical tools of a scene shop. People need to build costumes and wigs, using all the tools of a dressmaking shop. People need to manage the box office and house (audience), using people skills and accounting skills and management skills. People need to write the plays and act in the plays. Theatre is the perfect storm of left- and right-brained people working together to create something larger than any one of them could create alone. One body, many parts. All working toward one end.

My students and I developed a kind of theology of ensemble, calling students to lives of service as artists. Public perception of professional theatre is that it tends to be a place of large egos. I believe, however, that because theatre is by definition an ensemble art form, the best theatre requires being submissive to a larger good. Healthy submission to a larger good can only come out of an environment of trust and respect. In that environment, one can improve and grow by taking chances and risking failure. We work hard to create an environment that makes such risk-taking possible, even admirable. In this environment, we honor each other and the God we serve.

This kind of work needs both permission and invitation. Permission to enter into the work. Permission to risk failure. And then an explicit invitation to join in the work. The invitation cannot be assumed. I do not always know what I am capable of or in what ways I need to be nurtured. An invitation from a trusted mentor can encourage me beyond my imaginings.

Living Up to Potential

One of the ways my mother taught me to love the Bible was by speaking it to me in ordinary circumstances. When I settled a dispute between my younger sisters, Mom said, "Do you know what the Bible says about peacemakers?" I did not. "It says, 'Blessed are the peacemakers, for they shall be called the children of God.'" I remember that moment because it marked me, a freckle-faced, frizzy-red-haired stutterer, as a child of God. Who, me?

Sometimes I complained that I wanted to be some age older than I was. (This was always happening. When I was thirteen, I wanted to be sixteen. At sixteen, I wanted to be eighteen. At eighteen, I longed for twenty-one.) Mom finally said, "Listen to this verse from the Psalms." And she quoted Psalm 118:24: "This is the day that the Lord has made; let us rejoice and be glad in it." "Karen," she said. "You're wishing your life away. This day is precious. Live this day. How many days do you think you have?"

And then there was Luke 12:48: "For unto whomsoever much is given, of him shall be much required." (It was always King James.) This was given to me as a motivator, of course. I had been given much. Solid, loving family and strong biblical teaching. I was smart, adept with my music lessons. I had good books to read, food on the table, and a roof over my head. Those things did not come without consequence. I was to live up to my potential—the potential given to me by my circumstances, which were undeserved blessings from God.

The imprint on me as a child and then as a young adult was that the Bible was important enough to my mother that she knew the book. Really knew it. And that if I knew it too, it would form me. (At ninety-five years of age, my mother has large chunks of the Bible memorized and continues to memorize new material. But that is a different essay.)

Living up to my potential, though, proved to be an arduous task. Not only because it is hard work, which is expected, but because I am a woman and an actor in mostly conservative contexts. So the consequence of being "given much" and living up to my potential became fuzzy. It is in the church and among Christians that I have had the most pushback on my work as an actor: *if the work isn't winning souls, what is the point in doing it?* Or, *acting cannot be good for a Christian because it is too self-serving and is about the applause.* Or, *acting is simply pretending, which is a pretty childish, even unchristian, thing for an adult to be doing.* Or, *it's only entertainment, and face it, most entertainment is of the devil at worst and a waste of time at best.* Affirmation from the institutional church for such a seemingly frivolous thing has not been part of my experience.

Of course, I have thoughtful responses to these and other objections, and since the environment that creates such objections was familiar to me, I knew how to navigate it. I compartmentalized. The church I love and am committed to will never be able to fully affirm my work, and that will be fine, I thought. The church will claim and affirm my faith; I will find other places that will claim and affirm my work. And to be fair, I had Christian friends outside of the institutional church who affirmed my "secular" work as an actor. My friend Diane, a former missionary, attended a convicting play about sexual identity with me in Chicago and declared the work of theatre artists to be mission work. She went so far as to say that churches should be supporting theatre artists the way they support overseas missionaries, an idea that was inconceivable to me at the time (an idea I currently think to be brilliant, by the way). I was inspired by Wheaton College's Jim Young, who was a mentor to me during my graduate school years. He believed that theatre artists telling beautiful, complicated, devastating stories well could change the world. What higher calling could a person want?

So, I straddled two of my loves—the church and acting—because I had teaching to keep me focused and grounded.

Permissions and Invitations

When Jeff and I arrived at Northwestern College, we knew nothing of the Reformed Church in America (RCA), but we were quick studies, and we grew to love our adopted denomination. In the RCA, we found a home for both our faith and our artistry, and it was good.

I was first drawn to Tim Brown because of his preaching and because, when we were first getting acquainted, he was one of the few preachers or pastoral leaders who fully understood that worship and artistry, preaching and story, are intimately connected. That understanding paved the way for our work to intersect on many levels. Tim's leadership is about relationship. He draws people in. He makes himself vulnerable so that others can be too. I continue to be drawn to Tim because he gives me permission and invitation.

Permission comes in the form of memorizing and presenting Scripture with him. Once, Tim asked me to memorize a large portion of Revelation and present it with him in Western Theological Seminary's chapel. Who memorizes Revelation? What is the point of that? It was not a flawless presentation from either of us, but it proved my mother's, and Tim's, point. Having Scripture in your bones changes you because it changes your relationship with the words. I did not encounter the text of Revelation the same after that experience.

Or permission comes in the form of embedding artistry into a sermon. Once, Tim asked Jeff and me to come to the church he was pastoring to do a series of sketches we had developed. He built his sermon around those sketches, alternating portions of sermon with portions of our presentation. An out-of-the-ordinary endeavor to see what the artist and the preacher could do together on the platform.

The thing about permissions is that they expand. Tim Brown giving permission to one or two gives others permission. Permission to try something different for the sermon time. Permission to memorize and present large portions of Scripture. Permission to invest in the extended time it takes to try something out of the ordinary. Permission to imagine.

Invitation to use my skills in ways I hadn't imagined comes in being asked to join the seminary board of trustees when I am neither monied nor ordained. Or being handed Amos Wilder's book *Theopoetic: Theology and the Religious Imagination*, which Tim has just checked out of my own college's library, with the admonition to read it. Or being asked to co-teach a seminary course on preaching when I am neither preacher nor theologian.

Or (and this one is the defining act for me) a conversation in which Tim asks to be taught. He has watched someone online "perform" Scripture, and he knows it is not good, that it misses the mark. Tim wants to know why it misses the mark. He wants to learn the vocabulary to critique it. So he asks the theatre artist he knows. He invites the artist to teach the preacher. He invites the artist to lead with him.

It is not unusual for a church body to use artistic endeavor in service of the institution's programs. It is quite unusual for a church body to invite the prophetic voice of the artist so that the whole of worship may be changed. Tim Brown does the latter, and his permissions and invitations to me have made me bolder in both my faith and my artistry.

Tim's imprint on decades of parishioners, generations of students, and innumerable friends has changed our denomination and has furthered the gospel work we do together. He gives us permission to come alongside him, and then he invites us into depths we didn't know we were capable of.

This is his gift. It is his legacy.

CHAPTER 4

Brother from Another Mother

Fred Johnson

Only God, in the mysterious outworking of his divine purposes, and not without a little irony, could have orchestrated events so that the person who became a dear friend and one of the few men whom I refer to as my "brother from another mother" was the Rev. Dr. Timothy L. Brown.

The irony is plainly evident. Tim is White. I'm Black. The tortured racial politics and cultural neuroses that have poisoned the historical evolution of the United States suggest that I should've referred to someone from my own background, especially with regard to that artificially constructed social bugaboo called "race," as my brother from another mother.[1] Fortunately, and aside from how it serves his purpose for establishing his kingdom on Earth in the great *eschaton*, God's not impressed enough by America's historical racial misdeeds to let them alter the destinies he chooses for his servants.

For me, the blessing of being allowed to serve God, the blessing that my Master and Lord Jesus Christ (through the Holy Spirit) gave

1 The Free Dictionary defines "bugaboo" as "an object of often obsessive fear, anxiety, or irritation... a difficult or persistent problem."

me the good sense to desire God in the first place, was richly enhanced when he also let me know Tim Brown as my brother from another mother.

Still, what exactly does it mean to call someone "my brother from another mother"? One urban proverb asserts that "a brother is a friend God gives you" while "a friend is a brother your heart chose for you."

Regarding Tim Brown, both assertions adequately summarize the relational context of two men who, though born of different mothers, nevertheless feel bound to each other as brothers. The Bible, as usual, offers a better illustration when it recounts the connection between the future king David and Jonathan, whose father was Saul, the ruler of Israel.

Scripture notes that soon after David slays the disrespectful, loud-talking Philistine Goliath of Gath, a warrior whose taunts left "Saul and his troops...terrified" and caused them to lose "all hope" (1 Samuel 17:11, *The Message*). Saul meets with David, bringing Jonathan with him. "Jonathan was deeply impressed with David" and "an immediate bond was forged between them." (1 Samuel 18:1, *The Message*).

Jonathan "became totally committed to David," which included becoming "David's number one advocate and friend," eventually making "a covenant with him," which was symbolized by Jonathan's giving David "his own royal robe and weapons—armor, sword, bow, and belt" (1 Samuel 18:1-4, *The Message*). As the son and fellow soldier of the warrior-king Saul, Jonathan surely understood the value of a soldier's weapons. Their quality and quantity meant the literal difference between life and death in battle, so giving such articles to David symbolized the strength of their bond.

They were born to different parentages, molded by the peculiar circumstances God foreordained for their lives, and then at the Lord's appointed time, Jonathan and David come into each other's orbit, journeying together as brothers from *other* mothers. Their affection for and trust in each other presents an excellent ancient model of the friendship I've been blessed to enjoy with Timothy Brown.

Act One: "The Real Deal"

A few years after coming to Holland, Michigan, in the early 2000s, when I began teaching history at Hope College, my colleagues honored me with the privilege of being their faculty representative on Hope's board of trustees. New and still learning the culture and mores of higher education, which were so different from the shark-infested ecosystem I'd fled from at Aircraft Braking Systems, I kept my eyes and ears open to also learn about the ways and nuances of West Michigan.[2]

West Michigan is home to one of the most ethnically Dutch communities in the United States, and West Michiganders were proud of their Dutch ancestry and had been known to make statements like "If you ain't Dutch, you ain't much."[3] By the time I arrived, such statements had seen their better days and were being uttered mostly by those soon to be claimed by the grasping hands of time.

Predominately White, devout in the Calvinist tradition, conservatively aligned with the Republican Party, and perennially clobbered by long, taxing winters, West Michigan hadn't even registered as a thought for me upon finishing grad school at Kent State University in Kent, Ohio.

But when God pointed me in the direction of Hope College, my prior experience as a modern-day Jonah issued stern reminders that, while our ever-patient God may occasionally allow is creatures to deny, delay, or distort his plans, when all is said and done, God *will* have his way.

Rather than be subjected to another belly-of-the-fish experience, I chose to follow when God put my feet on the path to West Michigan, Hope College, and the school's board of trustees. There I met fellow board member Timothy Brown, who was also serving as Hope's dean of the chapel.

Tim was effusively joyful from just being around people, always ready to share a quick warm smile, and happily unable to contain Christ living inside him. But the features that *really* stood out about Tim were the passion, power, and precision of his prayers. The fervency of his prayers, the way they quietly cut through the façade of human pride and foible, and the gentle authority infused in their utterances often left me thinking, *This is someone who's seriously studied the way Jesus prayed.*

At the start of board meetings or when we broke for lunch and reconvened, Tim was always asked, and was only too glad, to pray. Before the board made a difficult decision or when discussions became too dynamic, Tim elegantly called time-outs by simply offering to pray.

2 Aircraft Braking Systems, known today as Meggitt Aircraft Braking Systems, was previously Goodyear Aerospace Corporation (a division of Goodyear Tire & Rubber).

3 See Michael J. Douma, "A Brief History of the Phrase 'If you ain't Dutch, you ain't much,'" July 7, 2019, https://michaeljdouma.com/2019/07/07/a-brief-history-of-the-phrase-if-you-aint-dutch-you-aint-much/.

The utter transparency of Tim's total self, on public display and not caring who saw or what was being thought as he appealed to God, exemplified his complete submission to the Lord. His simple prayer language recalled Scripture's description of the intimacy between God and Moses when it stated that "the Lord used to speak to Moses face to face, as one speaks to a friend" (Exodus 33:11).

Seeing a pulpit expositor of the Word being so comfortable in his own skin while yet speaking with such unshakeable certainty of God's grace, love, magnificence, wisdom, and power moved me to reinterrogate my own understanding of what it meant to be a servant of the Lord.

Growing up in the African American Southern Baptist tradition, I'd sat under the leadership of preachers who could shake the rafters when calling upon the Lord, especially when imploring him to lift the heels of contemporary pharaohs off the necks of his African American children. While not as widely known as praying, preaching, and teaching titans like Martin Luther King Jr., Ralph Abernathy, Fred Shuttlesworth, Gardner C. Taylor, Wyatt T. Walker, C. J. Franklin, Jeremiah Wright, and others, the country-born and -bred preachers of my childhood nevertheless moved parishioners to holy dance in the aisles.

Their thundering voices beseeched the great I Am for answers when, for their people, they cried "How long, O Lord? Will you forget me forever? How long will you hide your face from me? How long must I bear pain in my soul, and have sorrow in my heart all day long? How long shall my enemy be exalted over me?" (Psalm 13:1-2).

Whether laden with degreed credentials or bearing stripes and bruises inflicted by a country that had enslaved, deported, and, failing all else, spared no effort to keep African Americans confined in second-class citizenship, those powerful praying preachers took the writer of Hebrews at their word, approaching the "the throne of grace with boldness" so that their people could "receive mercy and find grace to help in time of need" (Hebrews 4:16).

As I grew into an impatient young adult, I rejected the mindset and methods of those robed prayer warriors, preferring instead calls for faster change like the October 29, 1966, gauntlet thrown down by Stokely Carmichael:

> We are engaged in a psychological struggle in this country, and that is whether or not black people will have the right to use the words they want to use without white people giving their

> sanction to it. And we maintain that, whether they like it or not," we are going to use the word "'Black Power' and let them address themselves to that; but we are not" going "to wait for white people to sanction Black Power We are tired [of] waiting; every time black people move in this country, they're forced to defend their position before they move.[4]

Born in Port of Spain, Trinidad, on June 29, 1941, Carmichael moved to the United States at age eleven. Watching his father literally work himself to death while pursuing the American Dream as a second-class citizen was one of many turning points that drew Carmichael into the Black struggle for civil rights.[5]

By 1966, fed up with the non-violent approach advocated by Martin Luther King Jr., Carmichael called for more aggressive tactics to achieve faster, wider-ranging results. He justified those calls by citing evidence from a shameful history:

> "It is clear that when this country started to move in terms of slavery, the reason for a man being picked as a slave was one reason–because of the color of his skin. If one was black one was automatically inferior, inhuman, and therefore fit for slavery. So that the question of whether or not we are individually suppressed is nonsensical, and it's a downright lie. We are oppressed as a group because we are black, not because we are lazy, not because we're apathetic, not because we're stupid, not because we smell, not because we eat watermelon and have good rhythm.... *We are oppressed because we are black*."[6]

Carmichael's historical explanation of the process by which the Gordian's Knot, or noose, of racism had been tied around the collective necks of African Americans found in me an attentive, searching student.

Before reading Carmichael's words, I'd recently finished Frederick Douglass's autobiographical narrative, which confirmed misgivings I'd been having about Christianity, especially its co-optation for crimes committed in the name of slavery. Such was the potency of

4 Stokely Carmichael, "Black Power," *Voices of Democracy*, University of Maryland, accessed January 5, 2021, https://voicesofdemocracy.umd.edu/carmichael-black-power-speech-text/.

5 "Stokely Carmichael," *Biography.com*, January 18, 2018, https://www.biography.com/activist/stokely-carmichael.

6 Carmichael, "Black Power." Emphasis in original.

Douglass's relentless condemnation of religion and its empowerment of professing Christians to perform acts of unspeakable barbarity that he felt compelled to distinguish his contempt for those persons from the life, work, and words of Jesus Christ:

> I have, in several instances, spoken in such a tone and manner, respecting religion, as may possibly lead those unacquainted with my religious views to suppose me an opponent of all religion. To remove the liability of such misapprehension, I deem it proper to append the following brief explanation. What I have said respecting and against religion, I mean strictly to apply to the *slaveholding religion* of this land, and with no possible reference to Christianity proper; for, between the Christianity of this land, and the Christianity of Christ, I recognize the widest possible difference – so wide, that to receive the one as good, pure, and holy, is of necessity to reject the other as bad, corrupt, and wicked. To be the friend of the one, is of necessity to be the enemy of the other. I love the pure, peaceable, and impartial Christianity of Christ: I therefore hate the corrupt, slaveholding, women-whipping, cradle-plundering, partial and hypocritical Christianity of this land. Indeed, I can see no reason, but the most deceitful one, for calling the religion of this land Christianity. I look upon it as the climax of all misnomers, the boldest of all frauds, and the grossest of all libels.[7]

Coming of age in the fading afterglow of the civil rights movement, whose boldest spokesperson for non-violent change had been slain by an act of violence, and trying to comprehend how the nation that had originally declared that "all men are created equal" while establishing systems, institutions, and attitudes that guaranteed inequality, left me doubtful and filled with simmering rage.

At fifteen, nearly being beaten to death by five officers of the gleefully bigoted Prince George's County, Maryland, police department; overhearing pledges of fellow U.S. Marines to kill "that nigger" (me) if we ever went to combat; and slogging through the endless psychic and spiritual grind of living in a land that had shown a remarkable consistency of indifference to the persisting socioeconomic, political,

7 Frederick Douglass, *Narrative of the Life of an American Slave* (Boston: Anti-Slavery Office, 1845). See also the online version at: http://utc.iath.virginia.edu/abolitn/abaufda14t.html.

and legal injustice inflicted upon millions of people of color—all this left me hyper-cautious about those making overtures of friendship.

Upon hearing Tim Brown's prayers, my own values were challenged about the rightness and fairness of dismissing him on the basis of judgments that I'd surely have found flawed and unfair if applied to me. But his openness of heart and spirit reminded me of what Jesus must have seen in Nathanael during their first encounter when the Lord exclaimed, "Here is truly an Israelite in whom there is no deceit!" (John 1:47).

Christ possessed the supernatural ability to take inventory and interrogate secrets lurking in the shadows of men's hearts, but I was limited to the evidence before my eyes, and it was disarming, because in Tim Brown, I found a stellar example of humility.

It was the kind of humility which I believe moved Christ to detect no "guile" in Nathanael and which recalled for me the enduring words of the Trappist monk Thomas Merton: "Humility consists in being precisely the person you actually are before God, and since no two people are alike, if you have the ability to be yourself you will not be like anyone else in the whole universe."[8]

Tim not only possessed the ability to be himself but, refreshingly, he was totally fine with me being *myself*. This was so much the case that the raw sincerity of who Tim was as a person dared the assumptions that molded and shaped "me" to disbelieve the persisting evidence of goodness that I kept encountering in my newfound friend.

The daily, seemingly effortless way in which Tim "walked" his "talk," especially his absolute belief in the *imago dei*, demonstrated Merton's meaning when he said,

> "It is not humility to insist on being someone that you are not. It is as much as saying that you know better than God who you are and who you ought to be. How do you expect to arrive at the end of your own journey if you take the road to another man's city" or "reach your own perfection by leading somebody else's life?" Because "it takes heroic humility to be yourself and to be nobody but the man, or the artist, that God intended you to be."[9]

Tim Brown possessed the kind of heroism of which Merton wrote. Brave and humble enough to be himself, he asked no less and

8 Thomas Merton, *Seeds of Contemplation* (New York: Dell Publishing, 1949), 60-61.

9 Merton, *Seeds of Contemplation*, 60-61.

no more of others, and he simply refused to let society's divisive rules on cross-cultural chasms matter in whom he chose to befriend. His open, inviting manner was not some expediently adopted behavior to check a box of religious correctness, nor a modified, mealy-mouthing compromise to just "go along to get along."

Tim's daily default to treat others with love, grace, dignity, and respect, irrespective of their origins, culture, language, or artificially imposed, divisive social insanities, which were rendered irrelevant by his consistent determination to make good on the Lord's commandment to love his neighbor as he loved himself (Matthew 22:39).

In Timothy Brown I'd found someone who was actually the person he advertised himself to be: a Christ-loving, people-uplifting leader of compassionate integrity who sincerely meant it when he looked upon this Black man and called me "brother." The day he hailed me as his "brother from another mother," I didn't balk, flinch, or doubt, because in Tim I'd not only found a friend and brother, but a brother and friend who was the *real deal.*

Act Two: "Go All the Way or Don't Go at All"

One day, on the first floor of Lubbers Hall, Timothy Brown (then dean of the chapel at Hope College) saw each other in the hallway. Along with some classrooms on the first and second floors, Lubbers houses the history, political science, philosophy, and English departments as well as the office of the dean of arts and humanities. As had become our custom, Tim and I waved and, speaking above the din, said something like "I see my brother from another mother."

We maneuvered toward each other through the milling students and professors who were leaving class and heading to wherever they were supposed to be next. While Tim and I exchanged pleasantries and caught each other up on our lives, the noise in the hallway slackened and the crush of people thinned to just me and Tim. There was a mischievous glint in Tim's eye as he leaned slightly toward me. "Dr. Johnson, I have a confession to make."

> "Speak your truth, my son."
>
> Tim started laughing, and so did I.
>
> "My confession," Tim said, "is that one day while hurrying to a meeting, I took a shortcut through Lubbers Hall. I was in a rush until I heard something that stopped me in my tracks."
>
> "What was it?" I asked.

"It wasn't so much 'what' but more like 'who.'"

I shrugged and waited.

"It was *you*," Tim said. "I heard *your* voice, echoing through the hallway. I followed the sound to the classroom where you were teaching and stood outside, mesmerized as I listened to an artist working his craft."

"Tim, encouragement like that coming from a master storyteller like you means the world."

At the time, Tim's life was settling down to some semblance of normalcy after he'd served as Hope College's Hinga-Boersma Dean of the Chapel while also retaining his position as the Henry Bast Professor of Preaching at Western Theological Seminary (where he'd been on the faculty since 1995). Serving the needs of both offices with the excellence required to glorify God's presence and mission in the lives of students, faculty, and staff at the college *and* seminary would've been taxing enough under normal circumstances.

Tim achieved that duality of excellence in a manner that justified the faith of Hope College president James Bultman who, regarding the search for a dean of the chapel, said, "There were several very qualified applicants from within and outside the campus community; but in the final analysis, the search committee recognized the exceptional gifts which Tim Brown [brings] to this position."[10]

Dr. Dennis Voskuil, president of Western Theological Seminary (WTS), underscored Bultman's assessment by observing that "Tim Brown possesses preaching and pastoral gifts which will positively affect the life of Hope's campus ministry program."[11]

Both of those stellar leaders were spectacularly correct, especially when considering how Tim's many God-granted gifts positively impacted me. For a long time, there had been a trend among some Christians to proudly exclaim "God said it, I believe I, that settles it."[12] This phrase caused me considerable angst as I pondered such a narrowly focused perspective in a world where, for example, some people had once believed that God approved of American chattel slavery.

While it might be "hard to criticize someone for firmly believing that the Bible contains God's instructions to the human race,"[13] the

10 "Tim Brown Named Dean of Chapel," *Hope College Campus News*, April 20, 2001.

11 "Tim Brown Named Dean of Chapel."

12 "God said it, I believe it, that settles it," *Dictionary of Christianese*, July 29, 2013, https://www.dictionaryofchristianese.com/god-said-it-i-believe-it-that-settles-it/.

13 "God said it, I believe it, that settles it."

historical record of humans' capacity for inflicting evil on others—and using the Bible to justify their cruelty—challenges the wisdom of such a notion.

Without knowing he was doing so, every time Tim Brown preached a sermon, taught a class, or gave a public presentation, he modeled the miraculous possibilities of transformation through the words of the Bible. This was especially so because he upheld God's sovereignty instead of using God as a hammer of ideological or cultural oppression.

Rather than being content to merely parrot Scripture and doctrine to display the accuracy of his memory, Tim demonstrated that serious Christianity required diligent learning, reflection, and discourse. This aligned Tim with the eminent Christian historian Mark Noll, who observed that

> Modern evangelicals are the spiritual descendants of leaders and movements distinguished by probing, creative, fruitful attention to the mind. Most of the original Protestant traditions (Lutheran, Reformed, Anglican) either developed a vigorous intellectual life or worked out theological principles that could (and often did) sustain penetrating, and penetratingly Christian, intellectual endeavor. Closer to the American situation, the Puritans, then leaders of the eighteenth-century evangelical awakenings like John Wesley and Jonathan Edwards, and a worthy line of North American stalwarts in the nineteenth century...all held that diligent, rigorous mental activity was a way to glorify God. None of them believed that intellectual activity was the only way to glorify God, or even the highest way, but they all believed in the life of the mind, and they believed it *because* they were Christians.[14]

"Diligent, rigorous" glorification of God neatly sums up the way Tim daily performed his roles of servant-leadership at Hope College and WTS. He did so partly through constant encouragement in word and especially deed, demonstrating the possibilities for a Christian believer totally surrendered to God.

While Tim was absolutely certain of the grace, mercy, goodness, and infinite power of the Lord Jesus Christ, he seemed just as certain that I was worth the time and friendship he kept pouring into me. Knowing what Tim detected in me that moved him to call me friend and brother

[14] Mark Noll, *The Scandal of the Evangelical Mind.* (Grand Rapids, MI: Eerdmans, 1994), 3–4.

remains a mystery. But the reality of his brotherly friendship kept me buoyed from 2007 to 2010, when I ran for Congress as the Democratic nominee in the Republican stronghold of West Michigan.

The decision to run did not come lightly or with speed because, until then, I'd been a political enigma wrapped inside a riddle cloaked inside a mystery. Planting my flag (so to speak) on a Democratic hill in West Michigan guaranteed the (figurative) drawing of knives and (literal) journeying into assemblies full of people who were in no mood to have someone not originally from West Michigan and obviously not of Dutch ancestry accomplish what would've been a seismic shift in regional and national politics.

By the end of my journey from novice candidate to seasoned politico, I'd experienced enough to fully comprehend the reason for Jesus' shrewd response when scheming hooligans attempted to entrap him:

> "'They came up and said, 'Teacher, we know you have integrity, that you are indifferent to public opinion, don't pander to your students, and teach the way of God accurately. Tell us: is it lawful to pay taxes to Caesar or not?' He knew it was a trick question and said, 'Why are you playing games with me? Bring me a coin and let me look at it." They handed him one. 'This engraving, who does it look like? And whose name is on it?' 'Caesar,' they said. Jesus said, 'Give Caesar what it his, and give God what is his.'" (Mark 12:13-17, *The Message*)

The odor of Jesus' impatience with such rank amateurs rises up from that passage in the Gospel of Mark like smoke from a burning fire. Likewise, by the time I finished my second campaign for Congress, my impatience regarding the chicaneries of politics had matured into a viewpoint perceiving a pox on both houses:

> The Democratic Party that had once been able to claim my vote for the mere asking had not only squandered it but lost something of even greater value: *my trust*.... Energized by beliefs I'd inherited as a child of the Civil Rights Movement I had gladly carried the Democratic Party's standard as a candidate in West Michigan's second congressional district. It was my turn to continue the work of earlier generations who'd struggled so tirelessly to harness the power of government for the benefit of all instead of just the privileged few. But by the time of my campaign, segments

> of the Democratic Party had morphed from being a champion of everyday concerns for working people everywhere into an exclusionary country club of high-priced consultants, smarmy name-droppers, and risk averse appeasers. More interested in celebrity photo ops than helping its hard-working supporters along West Michigan's lakeshore, the Party had atrophied into a routinely dismissed nuisance in the district. Months before election night on November 4, 2008, I finally comprehended that no matter how long, or hard, I and my staff worked. No matter the depth and breadth of our hopes and endurance, we were on our own. Aside from our symbolic value and the willingness of West Michigan's lakeshore Democrats to serve as a funding source for other campaigns across the nation, *...we were expendable.*[15]

It would be less than truthful to claim that losing two congressional races didn't produce feelings of anger and, yes, even a residue of bitterness. One of the many factors that helped me maintain proper perspective was Tim Brown's constant reminders that *real* hope resided in the grace, mercy, love, and power of the Lord Jesus Christ.

We never verbally jousted over policies, social issues, or trends, but Tim nevertheless made his positions clear, sharing his concerns by speaking the same truth to power in the same way Jesus did two thousand years earlier.

His affirmations replenished my emotional fuel tank when it was low. His prayers were reassurance that God's angelic legions watched over me. His concern for feeding the hungry, housing the homeless, clothing the naked, and seeing justice ultimately triumph over injustice intersected with both parties' proposals while exposing the fact that both were incapable of finding lasting solutions, which are only possible through the power of God.

So often, the grueling daily necessities of full-time campaigning were lightened by reminders of the excellence with which Tim performed his duties as Hope's dean of the chapel and as a professor at WTS. He confirmed that God didn't mind his children stretching themselves, taking on new challenges, and daring to hope for great things. Tim's casual achievement of excellence while supporting me reaffirmed that when human beings derive their motivation from God's inexhaustible Holy Spirit, nothing is impossible.

[15] Excerpt from Fred L. Johnson III, *Schmuck: A Political Awakening.* This book is currently being edited for publication. Projected completion is mid- to late 2021.

God, the ultimate cosmic recycler, took my experiences as a twice-failed congressional candidate and channeled them into pursuing a master of divinity degree program at WTS, which mean Tim became one of my academic instructors. With his "diligent, rigorous mental activity" in glorifying God as my professor, Tim underscored the possibilities God has in store for those who tell him, "Lord, I surrender."

I'd never been bashful about taking on large challenges (like becoming a Marine Corps officer, pursuing a doctorate in history, or running for Congress as a Democratic target in a Republican shooting gallery), but Tim Brown, elevated by God, presented a fuller vision of the manner in which the master of the universe wanted his servants to think, act, and live. Because God is not a half-stepping, partially decided, sort-of-committed Divine, and he prefers servants who are likewise all-in.

Tim demonstrated such servanthood, stirring in me a desire to be a like-behaving follower of the Christ and friend to others as Tim had (and has) been to me. This was not the "Tim Brown" method, but rather God putting his cosmic cards on the table, stating plainly that only *one* style of followership satisfies his expectations: *go all the way or don't go at all.*

Act Three: "A Standing Yes"

It makes perfect sense in a world filled with scam artists, hoodwinkers, bamboozlers, shade-throwers, snake-oil salespeople,, and the generally untrustworthy and unlovable to never, *ever* commit to be there for someone no matter what. Because in a world in which husbands and wives, parents and children, and friends have respectively failed to keep vows, proven that blood *isn't* thicker than water, and in which friendship is often dependent upon fair or foul weather, promising to have someone's back seems like foolhardy risk. And yet, this is exactly what I'd promised my "brother from another mother" Timothy Brown.

Like a check not yet cashed, Tim had my promise in his possession and, being a disciplined, wise steward, he hadn't frivolously withdrawn from its vaults of potential. Then came that week during spring semester of 2017, just a few days before WTS's commencement.

Eminent theologian and public intellectual Miroslav Volf was to deliver the keynote address on Sunday, May 8. Mere days before, Volf called Tim with apologies for having to cancel. His wife had suddenly taken ill. With his usual grace, Tim reassured Volf that he totally understood was praying for Mrs. Volf's swift and complete recovery.

According to Tim, what happened next came as easy to him as breathing: "I sat there wondering what to do next, and I instantly knew: 'I'll call Fred Johnson.'"

When I answered the phone and heard Tim's voice, the day's stress dissipated like morning mist fleeing the rays of an early sun. Along with the annual organized chaos of spring classes ending, giving and grading final exams, and reconciling incomplete committee work, Hope College was also preparing for its own commencement. The only difference was that Hope's was on Saturday while Western's was scheduled for Sunday. And on top of my overflowing plate of activities and responsibilities, my colleague Scott Vanderstoep and I planned to depart for Detroit early Monday morning with a group of students bound for Vietnam.

Our conversation didn't last long. Tim said, "Dr. Volf can't deliver the commencement address, and I thought, 'Hey! I know someone who'll be just as good: Fred Johnson.'"

Tim had only to state the need, and I said, "Yes!"

For a long time, I'd told Tim that he and WTS both had a standing "Yes!" from me. In the aftermath of my two runs for Congress, I enrolled in Western not so much seeking another degree but hoping to obtain some understanding of the purpose behind those twin exercises in futility. Also, while the researcher in me desperately needed God to answer "why," these words from Romans 8:28 kept rattling around my brain: "We can be so sure that every detail in our lives of love for God is worked into something good" (*The Message*).

Gently, and over time, my Master revealed that, while Congress had been a goal of *mine*, it had never been his plan for me (at least not at that time). He instead invited me into the community of WTS, where I forged new friendships and further honed my mind and skills with the sharpening tool of his Word.

I was also given the privilege of sitting under the teaching of Tim Brown. Our normally rich conversations expanded into new territories, strengthening the unity that resonated whenever either of us said, "You're my brother from another mother."

Ironically, it was that increased closeness which left me wondering about Tim's calling upon me to meet the challenge of Western's commencement crisis. I'd surely uphold the promise of my standing "Yes!" But standing in for a powerful scholar like Miroslav Volf coated my forehead with fresh perspiration. As my kin back in the DMV (D.C., Maryland, Virginia) area might've said, Miroslav Volf was *no joke.*

Born and educated in Croatia (as well as the U.S. and Germany) and serving as the Henry B. Wright Professor of Theology at Yale Divinity School (where he also founded and directed the Yale Center for Faith and Culture), Volf had written or edited more than twenty books and over 100 scholarly articles, and he'd been featured in esteemed media outlets like *The Washington Post*, *Christianity Today*, *The Christian Century*, *Sojourners*, and NPR. I'd written a few novels, co-authored a biography of the rapper Tupac Shakur, and was producing a growing list of Civil War–related book reviews, but my publishing record compared to Volf's needed more work.

Volf was also an internationally recognized scholar and an in-demand speaker who'd been called upon to share his views on matters of national and global importance. I'd occasionally flattered myself with hopes that, perhaps, some of what I'd shared with students might eventually be useful to them, but compared to Miroslav Volf, well...

Admonitions from elders about the perils of comparing oneself to others echoed in my ears, but as with Adam and Eve in the garden, the temptation to sample those problematic fruits of thought proved overwhelming. But just as he'd done during the drama in the garden, God stepped into the moment to take measure of the situation. On so many occasions in the course of my hard-headed, doing-it-my-way life, I'd left God no choice other than to correct me like he'd corrected King Nebuchadnezzar.

Along with getting too big for his kingly britches in Daniel 4, Nebuchadnezzar's self-exaltation risked having people think that perhaps God didn't have as much power over his creation as he'd claimed. After he was driven mad and banished into the wilderness for seven years to live like a beast, Nebuchadnezzar finally aligned his priorities with God's and had his sanity, kingdom, and power restored (See Daniel 4:1-37).

God seemed to be asking me, "Are you implying that I was mistaken in having my servant Tim call you for this assignment?" Translation: "Are you, like King Nebuchadnezzar, exalting your own judgment over *mine*?" The last hassle I ever want is for God to spend seven years making sure I know he's in charge.

Assessing God's reasons for having Tim request that I deliver the keynote at Western's commencement proved an interesting venture, but in truth, I would have done it anyway. For reasons satisfactory to Tim and the Triune God who'd moved him to be satisfied, I'd been deemed sufficient to complete the task on that commencement occasion, and that's all I needed to know.

I set about composing a keynote worthy of Tim's trust and confidence in me, then purposed to deliver it as only I, not Miroslav Volf, could. As evangelist Joyce Meyer once observed, "God will help you be all you can be, but He will never help you be someone else."[16]

On the designated day, at the appointed time, Tim Brown introduced me to the graduates, faculty and staff, and friends and family seated in the pews of Hope College's Dimnent Chapel. My heart was bursting with gratitude: first, to God for the privilege of speaking his Word to his people. Second, I was grateful to Tim for remembering my standing "Yes!" Finally, I was grateful that Tim had taken me at my word and allowed me a few moments to return the many gifts he'd given to me as my brother from another mother.

I wait expectantly for Tim's next call, because my enduring "Yes!" still stands.

Conclusion

In 1903, the brilliant historian, sociologist, writer, editor, and activist William Edward Burghardt (W. E. B.) Du Bois declared that "the problem of the twentieth century is the problem of the color-line—the relation of the darker to the lighter races of men in Asia and Africa, in America and the islands of the sea."[17]

The very recent history of the United States (for example, the 2017 alt-right rally in Charlottesville, Virginia, at which bigots chanted "Jews will not replace us!"; the forty-fifth president's constant naked appeals to racism and xenophobia; and the unconscionable devastation of the COVID-19 virus on communities and people of color) confirms and underscores that the "color-line" remains a potent "problem" for the twenty-first century.

The difficulty of bridging the gap between America's racial majority and minorities, especially the African American community, is further challenged by a long miserable history of Christian cooperation and/or co-optation of the kind that moved Martin Luther

16 Qtd. in John C. Maxwell, *Put Your Dream to the Test: 10 Questions to Help You See It and Seize It.* (Nashville: Thomas Nelson, 2009), 17.

17 W. E. B. DuBois, *The Souls of Black Folk* (1903; Project Gutenberg, 2019), chap. 2, https://www.gutenberg.org/files/408/408-h/408-h.htm#chap02.

King Jr. to once remark, "Nothing in the world is more dangerous than sincere ignorance and conscientious stupidity."[18]

Black theologians like James Cone were unsparing in their analysis and criticism of the contributions or indifference of White Christians in institutionalizing the racialized insanity of the evolving United States of America:

> "Unlike Europeans who immigrated to this land to escape tyranny, Africans came in chains to serve a nation of tyrants. It was the slave experience that shaped our idea of this land. And this difference in social existence between Europeans and Africans must be recognized, if we are to understand correctly the contrast in the form and content of black and white theology."[19]

Cone further noted that the "difference between black and white thought" on such matters was because African Americans "did not devise various philosophical arguments for God's existence, because the God of the black experience was not...metaphysical.... God was the God of history, the Liberator of the oppressed from bondage. Jesus was...God's Word made flesh who came to set the prisoner free" and "make the first last and last first."[20]

As was the case during the years before the Civil War, so it remains that America's racial strife re-invigorates the likelihood that, for African Americans, God's salvation, mercy, grace, and love will be seen through a prism of liberation. Then again, there's also the necessity to honestly acknowledge that the twenty-first century finds America in a better location than those years before the Civil War or when Du Bois made his dire prediction. Much work certainly needs to be done to move America and American Christians closer to the reality of the amazing eschatological gathering best described by the apostle John through the revelation God permitted him to see: "I saw a huge crowd, too huge to count. Everyone was there—all nations and tribes, all races and languages" (Revelation 7:9, *The Message*).

Such a time will surely come, but I am fortunate to have already experienced that great coming together of love, respect, and celebration of the Christ through the closeness shared with my brother from another mother, the Rev. Dr. Timothy L. Brown.

[18] Martin Luther King Jr., *Strength to Love* (Boston: Beacon Press, 2019), 39.

[19] James H. Cone, *God of the Oppressed* (New York: Orbis Books, 1975), 49–51.

[20] Cone, *God of the Oppressied*, 49–51.

CHAPTER 5

Monica and Macrina: Students of Scripture, Teachers of Teachers

Han-luen Kantzer Komline

It is my honor and delight to celebrate the ministry and scholarly service of the Rev. Dr. Timothy Brown by contributing to this volume. The essay that follows brings together three elements of Tim's legacy that have personally encouraged me, as well as countless others. The first is Tim's enthusiastic support for women in Christian ministry. Those who regularly heard Tim preach, as I did during my first five years as a faculty member at Western Theological Seminary (WTS), will doubtless have had occasion to hear him exposit biblical passages pertaining to women in ministry. To name just two examples, I recall sermons on Romans 16 and Luke 10:38-42 in which he drew our attention to how the Bible itself highlights and underlines the value of women's leadership. For Tim, upholding the authority of women in ministry was of a piece with his commitment to Scripture, the second element of his legacy I wish to highlight.

Tim loves the Bible and has been passionate about instilling this love in others, whether through teaching, preaching, in personal conversation, or in formal communications to the seminary community as president. Of course, Tim's own doctoral work, so important for shaping the ethos of WTS and generations of students who have entered its doors, also focused on a particular expression of this passionate commitment to Scripture: the practice of interiorization and its potential to enrich the worship life of the church. Perhaps it was partly his joy in interiorizing biblical wisdom, in addition to parallels with his own life experience of radical transformation by God and eventual decades of service in ministry, that primed Tim to connect so strongly with Augustine of Hippo. This brings me to the third element of his legacy that I salute in the contribution that follows: his admiration for the mothers and fathers of the faith who have gone before us and his eagerness to share their insights with younger generations.

To see Tim's dog-eared copy of *Confessions* is to witness the physical evidence of his affection for this classic text: it has been read and re-read, underlined and starred, memorized and quoted. Tim speaks with admiration not only of Augustine, but also of Ambrose, the great bishop of Milan whose renowned interpretation and preaching of Scripture helped to persuade Augustine of the credibility of the Christian faith. Tim's affection for *Confessions* represents his larger commitment to learning from the giants of the Christian past and to passing on their wisdom to future heirs of the faith, just as Augustine sat at the feet of Ambrose before he became the kind of person who could offer a work like *Confessions* to generations yet unknown.

In the following essay, I hope to pay tribute to these three aspects of Tim's ministry and leadership. By focusing on Monica and Macrina, fourth century giants of the Christian heritage who also happened to be women, I would like to honor Tim's celebration and support of women in ministry. To highlight their faithful and passionate service as biblical interpreters is to point to a second area that has been a constant focus in Tim's ministry as well, in whatever form it takes. And finally, by addressing the way the biblical interpretation of both Monica and Macrina expressed itself in their powerful teaching ministries, with an untold impact on future generations, I would like to incite in readers a holy ambition to have the kind of lasting impact that is made possible when God takes up the work of faithful servants such as Tim, who seek not only to appreciate Scripture for themselves, but also to instill in others a deep love and respect for God's Word. This essay, then, is written in a spirit of gratitude for Tim's unstinting and self-sacrificial gifts to unnumbered future leaders of the church, who, Lord willing, have and will themselves invest in and nurture new generations of disciples.

✠

"What are you doing?[1] In those books which you read, have I ever heard that women were introduced into this kind of disputation?" This almost awkwardly direct interjection comes from Augustine's mother Monica when she finds out he is recording her comments for his book *On Order.*[2] Instead of being honored, she is dismayed by the censure her inclusion may bring him. In response, Augustine concedes that some may dismiss him for including the voice of a woman in his writings. But he doesn't give a whit for such critics, he says; such "proud and ignorant men" should attend more to the substance and less to the "dress" of what they read.

Though he expects some superficially minded people will look down on him for including a woman's ideas, Augustine incorporates Monica's contributions because her ideas are so good. He wants her to be a part of the discussion because her spiritual inclinations and intellectual chops make her indispensable. He writes of his mother, "By long intimacy and diligent attention I had by this time discerned her acumen and burning desire for things divine.... Her mind had been revealed to me as so rare that nothing seemed more adapted for true philosophy. Accordingly, I had determined to do my best that she be not absent from our conversation" (*On Order,* 2.1.1). And so, through Augustine's account, we gain a precious glimpse of this brilliant mother of the church.

Of the few early Christian women commonly known among Christians today, Monica and Macrina are perhaps the most familiar. More than anything else, these fourth-century mothers of the church are famed by association—with Augustine, Monica's prodigal son turned father of the Western church, and with Gregory of Nyssa and Basil, Macrina's younger brothers, long known along with their friend Gregory of Nazianzus as "the Cappadocian fathers." These men who made Monica and Macrina famous shaped the theological imagination of the entire Christian tradition, giving classic formulation to doctrines we now consider basic: Trinity, grace, the Holy Spirit. Like Eunice to Timothy and Miriam to Moses (2 Timothy 1:5 and Hebrews 2:7), Monica and Macrina are great women of the faith who enabled

1 This essay has been expanded from a shorter version that first appeared in a special issue of *Christianity Today* published in September 2020. Overlapping material is used with permission.

2 Augustine, *On Order*, trans. Robert P. Russell (New York: Cosmopolitan Science & Art Service Co., Inc., 1942), 1.11.31. Hereafter cited internally.

the ministries of great men. Submission to the spiritual leadership, teaching, and admonition of Monica and Macrina, which continued well into the adulthood of both Augustine and Gregory, made these church fathers the giants they were.

But what can we say about Monica and Macrina as faithful biblical interpreters in their own right? In both cases, a lesser-known yet foundational aspect of their legacy, as depicted in the texts that come down to us, is their work as students and teachers of God's Word.

To ponder this dimension of their contribution, or, for that matter, to comment on these figures in any depth at all, requires relinquishing guarantees of absolute historical accuracy. As is the case with the vast majority of texts associated with early Christian women, the biblical interpretations attributed to Monica and Macrina do not come down to us in their own words, but rather in texts written about them by men.[3] Did they really say what Augustine and Gregory claim they did? We simply cannot know with absolute confidence. What Augustine and Gregory wrote comes to us in diverse literary forms, some of which—such as the philosophical dialogue, which will be featured in the analysis that follows—allow for license with historical fact.

At the same time, we need not overestimate the case for fictionality. Why assume, for example, that second-person narratives are any more or less accurate *per se* than first-person accounts? One can easily imagine a scenario in which such humble women as Monica and Macrina, especially under the pressures of their male-dominated societies, might be inclined—were they to compose a work describing themselves—to underplay and underrate their own perspectives. We should also bear in mind other factors suggesting the plausibility of what Augustine and Gregory say about their mother and sister. First, the broad circulation of their writings, including to those who knew personally the characters depicted, provided a kind of check against any truly outrageous characterizations. Second, given their social status, it is likely that both Monica and Macrina were literate, and

[3] Elizabeth A. Clark discusses the theoretical challenges attending the recovery of female voices of early Christianity in "Holy Women, Holy Words: Early Christian Women, Social History, and the 'Linguistic Turn,'" *Journal of Early Christian Studies* 6, no. 3 (1998): 413–30. Clark addresses the case of Gregory's construction of Macrina at length on pages 423–29. For a longer version of the essay, see also Elizabeth A. Clark, "The Lady Vanishes: Dilemmas of a Feminist Historian after the 'Linguistic Turn,'" *Church History* 67, no. 1 (1998): 1–31. A very similar discussion of Macrina can be found on pages 23–30.

thus enjoyed some of the associated intellectual privileges that would have equipped them as thinkers of the kind Augustine and Gregory portray.[4] And third, what Augustine and Gregory attribute to Monica and Macrina is internally coherent—broadly consistent across the different works in which they comment about these women.[5]

Furthermore, as illustrated by Monica's surprised exclamation verging on chastisement from *On Order* and the exchange that followed, male authors in some cases stood only to lose—not, as frequently the case today, to gain—by the inclusion of a woman.[6] Monica's presence was an optical liability Augustine was happy to disregard for the sake of intellectual substance gained; it was the exact opposite of modern-day tokenism. Why would he invent her contributions given the cost of attributing them to a woman?

At the end of the day, we cannot prove that Monica and Macrina actually did and said what Augustine and Gregory say they did. But neither can we disprove that Monica and Macrina actually had the insights attributed to them. We need to keep an open mind when it comes to our assumptions about the "historical" Monica and Macrina, while also acknowledging that Monica and Macrina as we know them—that is, as the literary creations of Augustine and Gregory—have

4 According to Gregory's *Life of Macrina*, Macrina was educated in the Scriptures from a young age. See *Life of Macrina*, 3.

5 Elizabeth Clark disputes this point. See "Holy Women, Holy Words," 423, where she points to Gregory's observations in his *Life of Macrina* about Macrina's exclusive education in scripture as rendering her philosophical expertise in *On the Soul and the Resurrection* implausible. Yet Gregory's *Life of Macrina* never indicates that her education excluded all philosophical texts and topics, but only that her education as a young child deviated from the usual, poetry-heavy curriculum, focusing instead on the biblical text. At the very least, Macrina's scriptural reasoning, which is the focus of the analysis that follows, is of a piece with the narrative and characterization of *Life of Macrina.*

6 Ever the clever rhetorician, Augustine *did* find a way to turn his disadvantage into an opportunity to flatter the intelligence and high-mindedness of his readers. He does not fear a drop-off in interest because of Monica, he explains, since his future readers are unlikely to be the type who care excessively about prestige, glitter and shine, given that they have already picked up the book despite its lowly author. Augustine implicitly congratulates his readers as a self-selecting group "for whom the fact that you [i.e., Monica] converse with me on the subject of philosophy will be more pleasing than if they were to find here something else of pleasantry or seriousness" (*On Order*, 1.31). Still, his defensiveness about keeping Monica's part in the dialogue suggests a real concern about being dismissed on this account. He also insists that "in olden times, women, too, have worked on the problems of philosophy." If there were no risk in including Monica, he would not go to such lengths to defend his decision. Though in a different sense than the one intended by Shakespeare, the theologian doth protest too much.

been and continue to be important for shaping how Christians have understood and imagined women as biblical interpreters.

Monica

Augustine characterizes his mother as a woman who prized and pursued Scripture in her everyday life. In a comic interlude in one of his early philosophical dialogues, he recounts how one of his pupils had recently learned a chant of Psalm 80:19. The young man could not stop singing it. He sang it in the morning. He repeated it all day long. He even kept singing, as Augustine put it delicately, when he had "gone out for the needs of nature." At this, Monica puts her foot down. She "reproved him," Augustine tells us, "precisely because the place was unbecoming for chant." The young man rejoins, "jestingly: 'As if, should some enemy confine me here, God would not hear my voice!'" (*On Order,* 1.8.22). To our modern sensibilities, Monica's reproof may come across as prim, or even a bit prudish. But this little anecdote, meant to amuse, makes a lighthearted gesture toward the enormous weight Monica accords the biblical text. She wants worship, and the Bible, to have a place of honor in the lives of those around her.[7] And this begins with mundane day to day rhythms.

In addition to respecting Scripture, Monica hungered for it. Augustine tells us in *Confessions* of her eagerness to hear God's word: "taking no part in vain gossip and old wives' chatter, [she wanted] to hear you in your words and to speak to you in her prayers."[8] Monica desired communication with God. As is well known, she confided her deepest hopes and longings in her Maker, pouring out her tears before him as she prayed daily, year in, year out, for the salvation of her son. But she also wanted to listen to God in his own terms.

One of the primary ways Monica did this was through regular Christian worship. Augustine tells us that Monica attended church twice a day "with unfailing regularity" (5.9.17). She was riveted by hearing the word preached by her well-known pastor, Ambrose (6.1.1). "She would zealously run to Church to hang on [his] lips, to 'the fount of water bubbling up to eternal life' (John 4:14)" (6.1.1). In a moment of

7 It is also helpful to bear in mind that while singing the Psalms may seem to modern readers a completely normal activity, hymn and psalm singing *in church* was only introduced by Ambrose to Monica's congregation in Milan during her lifetime. See *Confessions,* 9.7.15.

8 Augustine, *Confessions*, trans. Henry Chadwick (Oxford: Oxford University Press, 1991), 5.9.17. Subsequent citations in text are to this version unless otherwise noted.

crisis for her church in Milan, Monica stepped in as an informal leader, "foremost in giving support and keeping vigil, and constant in her life of prayer" (9.7.15).[9] Since the eastern tradition of singing psalms was introduced at Milan at this time, this likely involved prayer in the words of the Bible. For Monica, hearing the Word in worship was frequent, consistent, and life-sustaining. She waited eagerly for the Word of God.[10]

Monica's reverence for Scripture, her desire to hear from God, and her devotion to encountering Scripture in daily worship all demonstrate her commitment to listening to Scripture. Regular listening, in turn, had the effect of internalizing, or encoding, Scripture into Monica's mind and heart, from which it overflowed at crucial moments to bring not only her, but others as well, to moments of heightened spiritual awareness of truths about God, others, and themselves.

The famous vision at Ostia, in which Monica and Augustine together attained a mystical sense of God's presence in the midst of a conversation about eternal life, is the best-known example.[11] But it is far from the only instance in which Monica's patient and consistent listening to Scripture made her a source of spiritual wisdom.

Because Monica was an attentive and committed listener to Scripture, she was able to speak the truth of God's Word into the lives of others, not least of all into the life of her beloved son Augustine. Augustine recounts how Monica nursed him on the name of Christ along with her milk when he was but an infant. This early experience irrevocably formed his tastes. As an adult, he found that "any book

9 This is Maria Boulding's translation: Augustine, *The Confessions*, Works of Saint Augustine (Hyde Park, NY: New City Press, 1997). Chadwick's translation uses the term "leader" for *primas tenere*.

10 Gillian Clark observes that Augustine's characterization of the pious Christian as an "ant" who stores up spiritual treasures for herself through small repeated acts of faithfulness is an apt description of Monica: "See the ant of God: every day she gets up, runs to God's church, prays, hears the reading, sings a hymn, mulls over what she heard, thinks about it, stores within the grain collected from the threshing-floor. This is what people do who listen wisely: everyone sees them go to church and come back from church, hear the sermon, hear the reading, find the book, open it and read." See Gillian Clark, *Monica: An Ordinary Saint* (New York, NY: Oxford University Press, 2015), 83, where she cites Augustine's *Expositions of the Psalms*, 66.3.

11 Augustine describes this mystical ascent in language saturated with Scripture, and also suggests that the original content of the conversation included reflection on biblical statements such as those of Psalm 79:3 and 5. See *Confessions*, 9.10.23-26. Gillian Clark notes the contrast between the mystical vision shared with Monica in book 9, which is "full of phrases from scripture" and that of 7.17.23. See *Monica: An Ordinary Saint* (New York, NY: Oxford University Press, 2015), 115.

which lacked this name, however well written or polished or true, could not entirely grip me" (3.4.8). When he first read the Bible for himself, he was shocked by its primitive form of expression. Yet for all its lack of stylistic luster, its pull was elemental: in the end, Augustine could not resist it. By teaching him the name of his Savior, which she herself heard and read in Scripture, Monica primed him to love the book that she loved.

When her son reached adolescence, Monica again communicated God's word to him. Seeing him consumed by the heat of his teenage lusts, she tried to restrain him and warn him of temptation. At the time, Augustine dismissed her advice as "womanish" (2.3.7). But he later came to see that God was speaking to him through her admonitions. He prays, "I believed you were silent, and that it was only she who was speaking, when you were speaking to me through her. In her you were scorned by me, by me her son, the son of your handmaid, your servant" (2.3.7). Augustine here alludes to Psalm 116:16, "Truly I am your servant Lord; I serve you just as my mother did." As Augustine tells it, he eventually became God's servant by following in the footsteps of his mother, who—by virtue of first hearing God's word to her—was able to speak God's words into his life.

Monica continued to speak God's word into the life of Augustine in his adulthood and after he had become a baptized Christian, as recorded in another early dialogue, *The Happy Life*. At the conclusion of the dialogue, Augustine has just suggested that the happy life is knowing God, the three in one. On cue, Monica concludes with an allusion to 1 Corinthians 13:13: "This is without doubt the happy life, and that life is perfect toward which we can, we must presume, be quickly brought through solid faith, lively hope, and burning love."[12] At this point, Augustine wraps the conversation up, thanking all the participants. Now an adult and a committed Christian himself, Augustine gratefully receives God's words spoken through Monica. She gets the last substantive word of the conversation.

While, as Augustine's theology underlines for us, God's gracious gifts can never be reduced to a calculable, guaranteed *quid pro quo*, there is a certain biblical logic to a pattern we may observe in Monica's life, conforming to the dynamic described in James 4:8: "Draw near to God, and he will draw near to you." Monica listened to God. This brought

[12] See Augustine, "The Happy Life," trans. Ludwig Schopp, in *The Happy Life, Answer to Sceptics, Divine Providence and the Problem of Evil, Soliloquies*, The Fathers of the Church 5 (New York: CIMA Pub. Co., 1948), 84.35.

benefits. As we have seen, her faithfulness as a hearer of the Word made her perceptive spiritually. Describing Monica's grief over her wayward son, Augustine writes, "By the 'faith and spiritual discernment' (Galatians 5:5) which she had from you, she perceived the death which held me" (*Confessions,* 3.11.19). We also read that Monica had the ability to discern between true and false visions (6.13.23). This kind of spiritual insight ought to be construed less as an unrelated reward and more as a good intrinsic to genuine listening to the Word. One cannot really hear what the Bible is saying and fail to be spiritually transformed in the process. Yet the benefits that accrued to Monica, diligent hearer of the Word, extended even beyond spiritual perceptivity. Monica listened to God, but God also listened to Monica. In the words of Augustine, "you heard her, Lord."[13] God heard Monica's prayers on behalf of her son and graciously gave her the desires of her heart. As a result, generations of Christians have been able to hear her story as penned by Augustine.

Macrina

Just as for Augustine Monica is a teacher taught by God (*Confessions,* 9.9.21) to whom he entrusts himself as a "disciple" (*On Order,* 1.11.32), so Gregory refers repeatedly to his elder sister simply as "the teacher." In Monica's case, we learn from certain crucial anecdotes *that* Scripture was important to her as a teacher, and we can also deduce this from what we are told about her devotional habits. But the examples of the actual content of her biblical teaching are both fragmentary and few. Apart from the section at the end of *The Happy Life*, there is not much data available on the specific biblical passages that influenced her or *how* she reasoned based on them. The dialogue *On the Soul and the Resurrection,* in which Gregory poses critical questions levied against Christianity while Macrina defends it, renders the situation quite different in Macrina's case.[14] Beyond showing us *that* Macrina valued Scripture, it gives us a gold mine of data about *how* she employed it.

The dialogue begins with high emotion. Gregory has set out to visit his sister to convey the sad news of their brother Basil's death. But when Gregory first lays eyes on Macrina, he is shocked to see that she herself is not long for this world. After giving Gregory a moment to express his grief, Macrina "reproached me with the apostolic saying,

13 *Confessions,* 3.11.19. See also *Confessions,* 5.9.16: "Where she was, you heard her."

14 Gregory of Nyssa, *On the Soul and the Resurrection,* trans. Catherine P. Roth (Crestwood, NY: St. Vladimir's Seminary Press, 1993). Hereafter cited parenthetically in text by chapter and page following the form (chapter, page).

that we should not grieve concerning those who are asleep, because this emotion belongs only to those who have no hope" (1, 27). Her first words in the work, then, come from 1 Thessalonians 4:13, which she invokes to exhort her brother. But Macrina's use of Scripture to intervene in a situation of personal crisis is just one of the many ways she uses Scripture in this dialogue. From this point on, she moves beyond the sphere of familial counsel to apply Scripture to matters of Christian belief, acting primarily as a teacher of theology.

First, Macrina views Scripture as the benchmark for the content of Christian belief. It places constraints on which ideas can be accepted and which cannot. In her words, "we always use the holy Scripture as the canon and rule of all our doctrine. So we must necessarily look towards this standard and accept only that which is congruent with the sense of the writings" (3, 50). Yet Macrina models how precisely these constraints make possible constructive and critical engagement with extra-Christian and extra-biblical viewpoints. In the dialogue, she engages a wide variety of philosophical views on offer, but with a clear idea of the standard by which these views must be evaluated from a Christian perspective. In some cases, she rejects philosophical views, while in others, she receives them positively. What makes possible her engagement in both cases is having a "canon and rule," to use her own words, by means of which she can identify perspectives compatible and incompatible with the Christian faith.

Macrina does not hesitate to correct Gregory based on concepts found in Scripture. After Gregory has described how logic leads to the conclusion that "our mind is the same as the divine nature," Macrina patiently corrects him: "'Don't say "same,"' my teacher said.... 'This is another impious argument. Say, as you were taught by the inspired voice, that the one is *like* the other'" (2, 45). Here she draws on Genesis 1:26-27 to temper Gregory's incautious proclamation.

Macrina also uses Scripture itself to argue for the idea that Christians have permission to leave certain questions unanswered. Macrina sees Paul as introducing a key distinction: "The apostle says that he has believed this much, that the age itself was fashioned by the divine will, and whatever has come to be within it...but the *how* he has left unexamined" (9, 97). We can know *that* some things are true because Scripture tells us so without understanding *how*. This distinction liberates Macrina to avoid getting distracted by insoluble problems while focusing on the matters that God has equipped her to address.

Macrina takes a cue from the apostle about what is most important. She does not go so far as to claim that just because Scripture omits an explanation, we should too. But she does register where Paul himself, for example, determines that understanding "why" is unnecessary. In Macrina's view, we should not feel pressured to explain what Paul himself deemed extraneous. She does not read Paul's precedent as establishing a prohibition, but as giving *permission* to leave some questions unaddressed. This intellectual modesty can help on topics as disparate as the causes of creation and the origin of souls. Regarding the first, she states, "we shall follow the example of the apostle and refrain from meddling with the discussion concerning how each thing exists" (9, 98). Concerning the second, she pronounces: "our discourse has refrained from meddling with the inquiry concerning the *how*, because we suppose the answer to be unattainable" (9, 99).

Secondly, in addition to setting boundaries for belief and intellectual ambition, Scripture informs belief's content. Macrina uses Scripture in a variety of ways to reason to conclusions. She does so on the level of individual verses, deducing, for example, from Genesis 1:28 that reason should control the emotions since human beings were commanded "to rule over all the irrational creatures" (3, 57). She also draws inferences from the broader biblical narrative, for example by arguing based on various biblical exemplars (Daniel, Phineas, Moses) that emotions are neither bad nor good in themselves, but are up to us to use wisely (3, 60). Like many other early Christian thinkers, Macrina uses Scripture to interpret Scripture. In a particularly beautiful passage, she uses a wide range of biblical images to imagine what it might mean when Paul describes God as "all in all" (1 Corinthians 15:28; 7, 86). Someday, God will be our everything: "a place for the saints, a house, a garment, nourishment, drink, light, wealth, dominion, and every concept and name of the things which contribute to the good life for us. He who becomes all will also be in all" (7, 86).

Finally, Macrina uses Scripture in a way that is confident and assertive. She is calm and collected in the face of critics and feels no pressure to satisfy them or even answer them at all. At one point, Gregory expresses concerns about those who reject the existence or creative power of God. How should we possibly persuade people who reject such basic tenets of Christian belief as the truth of the resurrection? Macrina's answer: we should not even try. "She said, 'It would be more fitting to keep silent concerning these matters, and not to consider the foolish and impious propositions worthy of an answer, especially since one of the divine sayings forbids us to answer the fool according to his folly (Proverbs 26:4-5). He is undoubtedly a fool who, in the words of the prophet, says that there is no God (Psalm 13[14]:1)" (1, 33). It is not that Macrina does not care about such people. Her point is merely that Scripture liberates us to keep our peace in the face of their critiques. We should leave them up to God.

Instead of turning to the Bible reactively, attempting to force it to answer objections posed by critics it was never designed to address, Macrina begins with Scripture and lets it speak on its own terms. Gregory anxiously presses her to address objections to the resurrection: "Don't you know...how great a swarm of objections our opponents bring forward against this hope? At the same time I tried to tell her how many arguments are invented by contentious people to overthrow the doctrine of the resurrection" (10, 104). Though perhaps this self-abasing characterization serves his own larger rhetorical purposes in the dialogue, Gregory comes across as timid and distractible. Like the disciples on board the boat with Jesus who say, "Teacher, do you not care that we are perishing?" (Mark 4:38), Gregory's boat is easily rocked by the waves of skeptical doubts, even if he does not share them. He seems inclined to let the critics of the resurrection set the agenda.

But the unflappable Macrina has a different plan: "I think that we should first run briefly through what is set forth in various places by the divine Scripture concerning this doctrine." (10, 104). She then draws on a variety of passages to establish a solid basis for the idea (Psalm 103, Ezekiel 37:1-14, and 1 Corinthians 15:51-53, in addition to the words of the gospels). Only after discussing at leisure what the Bible has to say about resurrection does she hear Gregory out on the objections.

After Gregory has rehearsed his lengthy list, Macrina is unfazed. Even now, she does not force the Bible into the mold of these counterarguments but explains, "we shall take up their discussion in the following manner. First, we must understand what the aim is of the doctrine about the resurrection, why this is declared by the holy revelation, and why we believe it" (10, 113). Her attention remains fixed on discerning what the Bible teaches on this topic, not on worrying about whether it satisfies the objections and questions about the resurrection Gregory has posed.

In offering her final assessment, Macrina does not mince her words. "Truly we should recognize the superfluity and ineptitude of the objections, as we plumb the depths of the apostle's wisdom. He also explains this mystery to the Corinthians, who may perhaps also have made the same objections to him which are brought forward now by those who attack the doctrine to overthrow our faith. With his own authority he cuts short the audacity of their ignorance" (10, 116). The shallowness of the counter arguments Gregory has described is exposed, not by measuring biblical realities according to the terms of the resurrection's detractors, but by immersion in the depths of Scripture.

At one point in *On the Soul and Resurrection*, Macrina draws on a text Monica also invokes at the end of *The Happy Life*, 1 Corinthians 13. The ultimate purpose of human life, Macrina suggests, is not arrival but an endless increase in love, because God's beauty is unlimited: "But when the thing hoped for comes, all the others grow quiet while the operation of love remains, not finding anything to take its place." For both Monica and Macrina, Scripture helps us along with mundane issues of human existence: how to sing a psalm of praise to God, how to raise a child, how to engage with people with whom we disagree, what to think about our own identity, how to grieve for a loved one who is dying. But for both women, in the end, Scripture is more than a useful how-to manual of the Christian life. The Bible gives us a foretaste of the stirring beauty of our Creator, and the ultimate, glorious purpose of our lives that gives meaning to every minor concern: endless, joyful, delight in God.

CHAPTER 6

Woman Called by God

Gail Ebersole

As we celebrate the Rev. Timothy Brown's retirement, I have been thinking back on my own forty-three years of ministry. I too am moving into retirement and have reflected much during this time. Like Tim Brown, I also have been a minister in the Reformed Church in America (RCA). But Tim and I have taken different courses—he in the church and seminary, while my calling has been exercised in two evangelical ministries, Young Life and InterVarsity Christian Fellowship (the first thirty-two years were spent with Young Life). In this essay, I will share my story as a woman who spent her career in evangelical ministry and reflect on some of the broader challenges women like me face in ministry.

I am grateful for my friendship with Tim Brown, which resulted in an invitation to serve on Western Theological Seminary's board of trustees. I am also grateful for Tim's strong support of women in ministry. Sadly, I have faced many obstacles and challenges as a woman who rose in leadership in the evangelical parachurch world, and although I have not wanted it to be the case, my gender has often been an issue. Women have been and continue to be second-class citizens in evangelical settings.

As I grew up, my parents encouraged me to do anything I wanted to do. My Presbyterian home church in Richmond, Virginia, modeled that women could be in leadership. My mom was an elder even before the southern and northern Presbyterian churches joined together to form the PC(USA). The message I received was that if I used my gifts wisely to help others, the world was at my fingertips. It was not until I got involved with Young Life, first as a high school student and then in college as a volunteer leader, that I realized this was not universally true. I was not allowed to dream the same dreams as men or even to use the God-given gifts that were emerging in my life. I was told, "It's too bad you aren't a man, you would really go far." Hearing that repeatedly filled me with self-doubt and made me wonder what God's view of me was.

When I initially pursued a job with Young Life, I wanted to join the staff in my home state of Virginia. The regional director, who was in charge of hiring, sent me a letter saying, "Dear Gail, if you were a man, I would love to talk to you about a Young Life position in Virginia, but since you are not, please talk to a different regional director." I found a regional director in North Carolina willing to hire me, but I quickly saw that women were not given leadership roles. We were expected to reach out to high school girls and do chores like buying food and writing thank-you notes. There was even a manual on how to be a staff woman that included the suggestion to look adoringly at the staff man up front while he was speaking. There were very few role models, and if I was anywhere with another more experienced staff woman, I would eat up the time she might spend with me. I wanted to know how to do this job, and I wanted to be great at it.

I lived with the knowledge that if I were a man, I would have been more respected. When men asserted themselves, they were showing leadership. When I asserted myself, I was an aggressive troublemaker. Yet I felt called by God to this ministry. I wondered what God wanted for me and my Christian sisters and brothers. I felt confident that women can and should be an integral part of ministry, yet wondered at times where my confidence came from.

I ran into people quick to quote verses from 1 Timothy 2 about women not having authority over men or Ephesians 5 about the headship of men. (Strangely, no one ever quoted 1 Corinthians 11 and demanded I keep my head covered.) I read other interpreters who emphasized the broader affirmations of the gospel and verses like Galatians 3:28 about there being no male or female in Christ. These writers pointed to examples of women in leadership throughout the Bible, women like Sarah, Miriam, Deborah, Ruth, Hannah, Abigail, and Esther in the Old Testament and Mary, Elizabeth, Phoebe, Priscilla, and Lydia in the New Testament. I came to embrace a hermeneutic that emphasizes the entire counsel of Scripture as having more weight than a flat reading of one particular verse.

It makes me sad to see the Bible used as a weapon to exclude and oppress people. I am a ministry practitioner, not a biblical scholar, and I don't have the training or interest to rehash all of this debate. Obviously, I have come to the conclusion that God intends for women to be involved in every aspect of ministry. The sermon preached at my ordination was based on the story of the prophetess Huldah found in 2 Kings 22. Huldah's prophetic oracle gave the word of Yahweh to the King of Judah. The prophet in the king's court at that time was Jeremiah, so it wasn't like there wasn't a man available for the job. The narrative makes clear that Huldah spoke the word of God directly. Sadly, this is not a Bible story any of us grows up hearing.

Yet rather than just smoldering in anger, I decided I could do more for God's kingdom by befriending my brothers in Christ and walking alongside them on a journey of discovery. Even though I was single at that time and had men tell me I would never get married because I was out of God's authority, I plodded on. I learned that friendliness brought an openness to greater understanding, and I believe this decision has served me well over the years.

After six years on Young Life staff in the South, I realized that I was going to have to make a significant geographical move to be able to take the position of area director, the basic leadership position in Young Life. Although this role was usually offered to men after two or three years on staff, there were no women area directors in any southern states. Actually, there was only one woman area director anywhere in Young Life, and she lived in Iowa. I had one woman mentor tell me, "Gail, go to friendly territory." Realizing I was stuck, I moved to the Midwest. Providentially, I accepted the position of area director in South Holland, Illinois. The members of our local adult support committee attended three Reformed churches in the area. It was the first time I had heard of the RCA. It was also the first time I heard of Tim Brown. Although Tim had just left First Reformed of South

Holland to go to Christ Memorial in Holland, Michigan, his presence and ministry never left the hearts of members at First Church.

I knew no one when I moved to South Holland. Yet I knew that God went before me. I clung to the image from Exodus of the Israelites following the pillar of fire in the wilderness. The regional director in Chicago was far ahead of most of his colleagues in providing leadership opportunities to women and people of color. Despite much criticism, he made deliberate decisions to recruit, hire, and develop people others considered either incapable or biblically barred from leadership. There was much fear, especially a fear (grounded in reality) that donors and supporting churches would not give to fund the ministry of women or people of color. Later, I learned there were similar dynamics in InterVarsity, especially in the South, where much of the ministry was funded by the Presbyterian Church in America. One place the unfair treatment of women played out was in funding for women who came on staff single and then were married. They were told, "You're married now, you should no longer work; it is your husband's duty to take care of you."

I began to spread my wings in the south suburbs of Chicago. There was open space to lead, and I was encouraged to excel and use my gifts. I am forever grateful for that opportunity. Many of the adult committee members who served as my "cheerleaders" are still dear friends thirty-five years later. The move helped me lean more fully into who God had created me to be. While I had been trained by a wonderful area director in the South, the culture did not accept women in leadership. In the Midwest, there was a culture that allowed women to flourish, and even more than that, I found men who were advocates instead of enemies. I was given opportunities to try things and grew immensely over the decade I spent as an area director in the Chicago region. I was able to stop projecting a façade and trying to do everything like a man would. I was never going to be one of the guys, so why try? Sure, I wondered at times if opportunities would pass me by if I presented my authentic self instead of who I thought I was supposed to be. But with a chorus of cheerleaders and some courage, I learned to live into my true self. It has been a long journey without a clear destination, but I have learned that being true to yourself is a primary way not to be afraid.

At that point, Young Life had existed for forty years, but I was often a pioneer. Being the first woman allowed to do something in Young Life's ministry meant I carried not only the weight of my own anxiety but, in a sense, the future of my gender. For example, I was the first woman to lead singing at two different Young Life camps, and on both occasions I had to fend off men telling me, "If you don't do well, a woman will not be asked to lead music for years." I was petrified by the time the music started, because even though I didn't like it, I knew those men were right. It was an impossible double standard: there had been many poor male song leaders yet other men still were allowed to lead, but if I turned out to be mediocre, *all* women would be set back. (On one occasion, as if by divine intervention, all the male song leaders at camp came down with laryngitis and lost their voices! I got to lead that whole week.)

Later in my career, I was invited to give the message on the last night of a Young Life camp. A woman had never spoken at camp, much less on the last night, which had extra significance because high-school students who had begun new lives in Christ were about to head home. Once again I was petrified, but by the end of the evening, I was infuriated. A fellow staff member who had brought a bus load of kids to camp had instructed his guys to turn their backs to me as I spoke. I was simply speaking about God's love. It was unnerving. I survived primarily by turning my anger into pity and sorrow for the narrow-mindedness and short-sightedness of that man, and I felt sorry for the sexist impact he had on the boys he'd brought to camp.

After eight years as the area director in the south suburbs of Chicago, the regional director job opened up. I was convinced that I was the most qualified person in our region and should be considered. The process was complicated because of some chaotic politics going on in Young Life. Our Midwestern vice president, who supported women's leadership, had been forced out. A new vice president from Virginia had signaled he was going to make a number of changes. Word was that he was bringing in people to "fix" the Midwest and had already chosen someone for Chicago. There was a national leadership meeting going on where much of this was being discussed. (I might add that only five of the one hundred people at that national leadership meeting were women.) There was so much pain and mistrust everywhere and I felt like this meeting might well mark the end of my Young Life career. One evening, after a worship service where I did not take communion, I was confronted by the new vice president. He said he was shocked that I would not take communion and said that "people will think you don't love Jesus." My love of Jesus had not entered into my thinking, and I couldn't care less what conclusion anyone else drew about me.

I was extremely angry and sad and felt sure that if I got up to take communion I would fall apart emotionally. As I expressed myself, I raised my voice. He also raised his voice. Soon we were standing toe-to-toe, more or less yelling at each other. I brought up how painful it was that I wasn't at least interviewed for the regional director job. He kept dancing around this, and finally I grabbed him by the shoulders and shouted, "I just want to bang this into your bald head!" Needless to say, I went to bed that night certain I was going to be fired. Amazingly, he came up to me the next morning at breakfast and said I was going to be the regional director. I was beyond stunned! Apparently, standing up for myself proved to him that I was a good leader.

I'd had an equally odd experience with this man five years earlier that was some mix of farcical comedy and tragedy. Still wanting to return to my home state of Virginia, I asked him to consider interviewing me for an open position there. He said no, and then added, "What would you do when all the guys go play basketball?" That was such a strange comment. I was tempted to sarcastically say, "Grab some pom-poms and go cheer," or maybe, "Get the snacks ready for when the boys finish." Instead, I told him I'd be fine having some time to myself and added that I was used to it because my father had been a Division I NCAA football coach. I could sense his estimation of me rising when he learned my dad had been a college football coach.

A decade later, I became the first woman (and still one of only two in Young Life's eighty-year-history) to become a senior vice president. At least this time I was told I could apply for the position, though I was also told that the competition was stiff and I should not get my hopes up. Again, I felt I was the right person for the job, yet I also knew I had to interview one hundred percent better than the two male candidates to get it. The other candidates came from different parts of the country, and I was the only one who had real knowledge and experience in the Midwest. I did homework on every state and noted places where there was no Young Life ministry. I spoke passionately about the potential of the Dakotas and the pain of young people in cities like Chicago, Detroit, and Milwaukee. Neither of the other candidates had ever stepped into these cities. I was chosen for the job. I had eight great years in that role, and what I enjoyed most was that my rise became a symbol of hope to women throughout Young Life. When I left Young Life, I took a similar position with InterVarsity, where I have served for the past decade. Happily, I did not experience at InterVarsity what I'd experienced at Young Life.

Reliving these traumatic stories has made me wonder how I or any woman working in the evangelical world persisted. I think of a gifted friend who was hired into a Young Life direct ministry position and was then introduced by a male colleague as his "sexetary." That would result in a harassment complaint today, but in those days we simply bore it, not wanting to rock the boat.

There were many women who served Young Life before me. That generation of women sacrificed much, and they are left with deep scars. They had doors slammed in their faces, doors which women in my generation were able to walk through. There probably should be a recovery group for women who had to fight so much to gain entrance into Christian "boys clubs." I am grateful for those who went before me and owe them much. I am also grateful for the men who were my advocates in Young Life, InterVarsity, and the RCA.

It is difficult for me to believe that there are still controversies over the role of women in the church. Antagonistic views divide the body of Christ, leading many hurt and bitter people, both male and female, to leave the ministries to which God had called them.

I mentioned that I became aware of Tim Brown when I moved to South Holland. The first time I heard him speak was at a gathering of Young Life area directors. Tim has been a favorite speaker at many Young Life gatherings for the past couple of decades. On this night, I watched 200 Young Life staff listen with rapt attention as he spoke with passion and used Scripture in a way they had never experienced. He told a story about hitchhiking across the United States with his brother. He was honest and vulnerable and shared from his heart about deep pain in his life. Tim had the courage to be who he was and not cover up his pain. It was a great example of authenticity. Being true to yourself means being willing to speak up on some occasions despite the fear of how you might be perceived. This is more complicated for women than for men, because "courageous" gets renamed "pushy." Yet as I reflect on a career in ministry, there is no doubt that being your authentic self is the key to longevity.

I greatly appreciate Tim's support for women in ministry, and although I know there are still pockets of resistance, I am glad overall that women students at Western Theological Seminary (WTS) don't have experiences like I had. I was reticent when I sought RCA ordination in the late 1980s because I was in a conservative classis, and I doubt I would have been taken under care if I had been seeking a role as pastor instead of "specialized ministry." I never would have gone through the process without the encouragement of the pastor in my RCA church. Although several pastors knew me because of my Young Life work, I still imagined picketers showing up on the day of my ordination. I made it through. As in my experience in Young Life, there were men who made it difficult and men who supported me. Tim has been one of the supportive voices, and I am grateful for that.

During my seven years of service as a WTS trustee while Tim was president, I saw him encourage and welcome many young women to the seminary. It has been exciting to attend chapel services and see the many gifted women students that have chosen Western. It's wonderful to see young women trust their intuitions and the inner voice that prompts them to embrace a calling in ministry. Those young women see other women in a multitude of professional roles at the seminary as staff, faculty, and administrators. Women scholars at Western are top-notch, have books released by major publishers, and are respected throughout the church. I applaud the supportive community that has been developed at the seminary. As a board member, I know there have been bumps along with way, but overall the climate is good and much different than what I encountered over the years. I applaud Tim Brown's work to develop this sort of culture at Western and believe this is a significant part of his rich legacy.

CHAPTER 7

The Project

Trygve D. Johnson

So faith comes from what is heard and
what is heard comes through
the word of Christ.
—Romans 10:17

Introduction

A personal calling from God is a mysterious instinct. It is hard to describe, or even talk about, without sounding a little presumptuous. God calls someone to specific work or vision? A personal calling is the sense that your life is directed by God toward a particular purpose—to serve an end that is not your own. It is the tacit feeling that your life belongs to something larger than yourself. A calling begins as a kind of whisper in the soul that if ignored or disobeyed would be a violation of one's best self. There is not only one calling. There are many different kinds of callings from God. For some, a calling is found in a relationship, or in a life dedicated to scientific research, or in giving one's life over to an artistic pursuit, public service, activism, or parenting. For me, God's calling was experienced as a pull towards a vocation in Christian ministry.

Specifically, I felt God calling me to be a preacher—a servant of his Word. This was a deep-seated conviction that I began to name when I was a young adult. Nevertheless, I resisted this narrow vocational path. Who would want such a burden? I prayed, "Lord, can I do anything else? Can I be an architect, or a history professor, or a lawyer—something a bit more culturally palatable?" Of course, the answer was yes. A calling is not fatalism. I could have pursued many different careers. God's love offers the liberty of choice. And still, in the end, like Jonah running from Nineveh, there was no peace or freedom in my soul until I let go of my objections and allowed the currents of the Spirit to carry me toward this peculiar and strange missional work called preaching.

If I'm honest, I feared God's calling on my life (and still do). As a young man, there was so much I didn't have a handle on (and still don't). I didn't know how to think about what it meant to be a pastor or to preach. I didn't grow up in a blue-blood ministry family, and frankly I didn't know many preachers, and those I did know I had a hard time identifying with. And growing up in the Pacific Northwest—what is now known as the "None Zone" (where people more often check "none" as a religious identity)—there was little Christian culture or institutional infrastructure to encourage Christian ministry as a worthy vocation, or even a normal one. Talk of being "called" into Christian ministry was odd in my world.

I also doubted myself. I was self-aware enough to know that I had a sincere faith but not a formed one. I questioned my emotional maturity and spiritual readiness. I worried what a life in ministry would mean for my identity. I was reluctant to be seen as a metaphor for a decaying religious establishment or be viewed as a mere vendor of religious goods and services, like some opportunistic TV evangelist peddling God to the masses for profit or recognition. I had enough sense that both of these paths were to be avoided. I was stuck. I didn't know how to pursue this calling while not turning into someone I didn't want to be. I intuitively knew that to be a pastor required a wisdom beyond myself, and that if I was going to do this kind of work then I was going to need help. I prayed for someone to show me a way forward.

What I needed was a teacher. I needed a guide to orient me to this odd vocation of talking about the ineffable mystery of God, someone to show me how to open a strange new world with a charged imagination, so that others may be invited to discover and explore the expansive geography of the kingdom of God for themselves. I needed a mentor who could teach me the old ways for a new day.

I was fortunate. The Rev. Dr. Tim Brown was that teacher for me. He provided a model of both what a pastor is and what preaching can be. Dr. Brown was a professor of preaching for over two decades at Western Theological Seminary, and for three years from 1996 to 1999, I had the privilege of being one of his earliest students. I learned more from Dr. Brown than any other professor I ever had. In the classroom, he was full of spiritual and scholarly insight. Yet the most valuable lessons I gleaned from him were not in the lecture hall, but rather experiencing him in action from the pulpit. Though a professor of preaching, he was still a working gospel preacher. He practiced the craft he taught others. Dr. Brown was the teacher I needed and had prayed for.

What I reaped from Dr. Brown, I have tried to sow into in my own ministry. Not just to emulate him, but to honor the wisdom God showed me through him. He showed and taught a distinct way of approaching the mission of Christian proclamation. This vision gave me a model that helped me avoid becoming a peddler of religious goods or being defined by an anxious and tight-collared clerical professionalism. He showed me that preaching can lead to freedom, that when the sermon is put to heart, beginning with internalizing the Scripture, and when each word is carefully selected, prayed over, and offered in hope for a people you are charged to love like a shepherd, God can draw us out into a wild place from which we can never return the same. For in that place we find the risen Son, Jesus Christ, and in him our true humanity is restored and redeemed.

The Bible was always the reference and Jesus Christ the subject of each sermon. Dr. Brown's style was not for all. But for me it was not only a gift, it was a revelation. A Tim Brown sermon was the best of a theopoetic expression, requiring of the preacher the imaginative skill of an artist, the mind of a theologian, and the heart of a pastor. Later, I would describe the vision of preaching I learned from Dr. Brown as *The Project.*

Inspired by the example and teaching of Dr. Brown, *The Project* is born out of a deep love for the risen Lord Jesus and his body, the church. It is a practice of preaching taken up to renew the church through a particular way of engaging with and proclaiming the gospel in preaching. *The Project* is an attempt to preach guided by the deep commitments of the pastoral calling that were inspired by the ministry of Dr. Brown.

Project is an acronym for these commitments: *Prayer*, *Remembering*, *Orality*, *Jesus*, *Exegesis*, *Conversion*, and *Tradition*. Faithful preaching begins in *prayer* by *remembering* the story of God and *orally* proclaiming *Jesus Christ*, through Biblical *exegesis* that offers a sermon with an eye towards *conversion* and finds a through line in connection with a theological *tradition*. In this chapter, I want to invite you to explore *The Project* and to consider joining this loose fraternity of women and men, old and young, who enter the pulpit each week to proclaim, without shame, the mystery of our faith: *Christ has died, Christ has risen, Christ will come again!*

The Project believes Christian preaching is essential for the vitality and continued renewal of the church. It is a vocational vision for pastors that encourages the cultivation of healthy congregations through preaching the gospel with a confident conviction in God's primary work of Jesus Christ, crucified, resurrected, and ascended, who is revealed in the Word and demonstrated by the preacher's interiorization of Scripture. A motto for *The Project* might be borrowed from P. T. Forsyth, who opened his Lyman Beecher Lectures at Yale in 1907 by saying, "It is perhaps an overbold beginning, but I will venture to say that with its preaching Christianity stands or falls!"[1]

This may sound romanticized given our weekly experiences of preaching—or if you are a preacher, our own sermons! Most preachers who are in the church and believe in the ministry of proclamation (there are many who do not) know tacitly that the church, like humanity itself, is both beautiful and terrible, a community of saints and sinners. And the chief among them in the Church is the pastor! Yet it is the pastor's job, despite their own faults, to stay attentive to God and to call others to do the same.[2]

One of the ways a pastor keeps people attentive to God is by inviting people to listen to the expounding of the Word in a sermon. The

1 P. T. Forsyth, *Positive Preaching and Modern Mind*, 2nd ed. (Eugene, OR: Wipf & Stock, 2007), 3.

2 See Eugene Peterson, *Working the Angles* (Grand Rapids, MI: Eerdmans, 1987), 2: "The biblical fact is that there are no successful churches. There are, instead, communities of sinners, gathered before God week after week in towns and villages all over the world. The Holy Spirit gathers them and does his work in them. In these communities of sinners, one of the sinners is called pastor and given a designated responsibility in the community. The pastor's responsibility is to keep the community attentive to God."

goal of any sermon is to reorient our visions and redirect our disordered affections back to God. This is why preaching has historically been one of the primary ministry responsibilities of a pastor. But how shall one preach if one is called by God to this duty?

This essay is written to offer one possible answer to this question, inspired by the teaching and witness of Dr. Brown. Here I try to synthesize some of the habits of preaching we try to practice in *The Project,* which have been tested and found to bear fruit.

P is for Prayer

The P in *Project* is for prayer. The sermon begins and ends with the preacher praying.

The first preaching class I ever took was with Dr. Brown. The class began a lesson I never forgot. There were about thirty-five of us in the class. Dr. Brown entered the class and looked at us. Then he smiled, said, "follow me!" and walked out of the classroom and down the hall. We looked at each other and then dutifully followed our professor down the hall. We were led into Semilink Hall, where Dr. Brown had arranged a chair for each of us in a large circle. Without saying a word, Dr. Brown knelt in front of one of the chairs and got on his knees and started praying. We all followed his example. We each knelt down on our knees in front of a chair and started praying. This, I learned, is where preaching begins. The preacher begins every sermon—the entire process, from text to finished sermon—on our knees. The Word preached is never before the Word prayed. We begin the sermon on our knees or we are merely talking.

What was notable about Dr. Brown's praying is that he did not speak. He was silent. What he was teaching us is that the prayerful preacher begins in silent listening. Prayer is not about us asking for things or even speaking. Prayer is an unceasing dialogue with God where we are always listening, attentive to God's presence in the present. Prayer cultivates in the preacher a disciplined disposition in which silence is the forerunner to speech, listening is the context of our proclamation, and solitude before God is chosen over the crowded sanctuary. Conversation with God in prayer is what we were made for.

Prayer is not for the faint of heart. It forces us to put our soul bare before the living God. There is no more significant practice to the preacher than work of prayer. We have to open up ourselves to God—our lives, our desires, our sins, our hopes—and bring them to God in an authentic and dependent posture of prayer. This is a posture of dependence on the sovereign God. Beginning the sermon on our knees puts our preaching before the true gaze of the loving God, whose Word melts away our ego and pretension like a block of ice in the summer sun.

This is why *The Project* begins with learning to listen to God through what God says in Scripture. Good conversation requires more listening than speaking. If prayer, then, is a kind of conversation with God, then learning to listen to God is a significant discipline. It is out of this biblical context that we join into an ancient and ongoing conversation between God and humanity. But this kind of conversation requires some training. We have to learn how to listen to God's people praying—how they use language, putting words to experience—and discover for ourselves how to enter into and participate in the deep prayers of God's Word, Jesus Christ, who is at the right hand of God and who prays without ceasing, in the Spirit, with sighs too deep for words (Romans 8:35). By learning how to pray what Jesus prayed, we learn to do our praying in Jesus' name.

To learn the language required for conversation, we have no better teacher than the prayer book of the Bible, the Psalms. The Psalms are 150 prayers that teach us how to listen to God, the world, and ourselves. The Psalms are the language that gives our prayer a cadence and rhythm. The Psalms are always where we begin to learn how to pray.

Praying the Psalms is a gift to the preacher. The Psalms teach us to pray with honesty. The Psalms are raw, vulnerable, human. The Psalms teach us that it's okay not to be okay. These 150 prayers give us a language and a vocabulary that directs our every emotion and bends them back toward the living God. They speak directly for us in the presence of God. Dr. Brown taught that "the best words to pray to God is God's own Word back to Him." Of course, he was channeling the wisdom of John Calvin, one of the greatest pastoral preachers of the Psalms, who believed them to be "an anatomy of all the parts of the soul," drawn "to the life, cares perplexities, in short, every disposition of the heart, with the blessed exception of hypocrisy."[3]

To pray the Psalms is a training in humility before God. We learn that the circumstances and feelings that we think so unique are not actually new to the human experience. In fact, we even have a way to pray about every emotion and pain without being afraid of their emotional

3 John Calvin, *Commentary on the Book of Psalms,* trans. James Anderson (Grand Rapids, MI:: Eerdmans, 1949), 1:xxxvii.

intensity. Thus, the Psalms serve us in prayer as tools to help us become more human before God, others, and especially ourselves. "Prayers are tools," writes Eugene Peterson, "but with this clarification: prayers are not tools for doing or getting, but for being and becoming."[4] Praying the Psalms helps us not to know more about God, but rather to form us into those who can be more *for* God.

The Project begins in prayer so that the holy conversation opens our eyes and gives us a clear vision of the expansive geography of God's reign and work. This holy awareness and relational attentiveness is where preaching begins. Ultimately, that is because the goal of the preacher is not a sermon. Rather, the goal of the preacher is to be confronted by the living God who makes a claim on every square inch of our lives. To pray the Psalms is essentially a relational conversation in which we learn that despite any circumstance we may face, God has given us the language to pray with confident conviction, in order that we find ourselves participating in the intimate and expansive prayers "in Jesus' name."

This is what Dr. Brown was inviting us to learn in my first preaching class. He wasn't inviting us to begin preaching on our knees, but to begin learning how to pray the Word, so that the words of the Word might be heard again and again for a new generation. *The Project* begins with prayer, for in prayer we begin with God.

R is for Remembering

The R in *Projec*t is for remembering. The sermon that begins on the knees continues with a learning by heart, for all true knowing is a knowing by heart.

One of the distinctive gifts of *The Project* is the work and witness of remembering. Memory is the soil where faith grows deep and tall. It is the human and emotional archive of the pulpit. The preacher's job is to remember the story of God, while at the same time remembering the story of the particular people who are hearing the sermon in their particular place. Central to *The Project* is the work of remembering and internalizing Scripture to shape the pastoral imagination for the people of God.

I learned the power of remembering Scripture from Dr. Brown. In a Tim Brown sermon, the listener is caught up in the event of recalling Scripture from memory. The Bible is not read, it is embodied. Verses

4 Eugene Peterson, *Answering God* (San Francisco: Harper One, 1989), 2.

of the Bible are not wrenched from the story and then applied out of context. Rather, what is impressed upon you is how the Bible's verses worked together to display the larger picture of God's promises. There is a significant difference between hearing the Word of God recited from memory and hearing it simply read. Much of the Bible, it must be remembered, would have been spoken first and then recorded. As Amos Wilder writes in *Early Christian Rhetoric,* "The uncalculating oral speech and dialogue of Jesus and his first followers gave place in part to memorization and repetition, and eventually to writing and later to the greater formation of publication."[5] The Bible was written in an oral world, where the primary means of sharing information and knowledge was through the spoken word. By retelling stories of the past, the community internalized the story in its collective memory.[6]

In the effort to take seriously the place of memory in Christian practice, Dr. Brown believed that Scripture should not simply be read, but internalized and then spoken freely from the memory of the heart. The power of remembering allowed his sermons the spontaneity to follow the contours of the text without forcing a prescribed message. Consequently, his witness of remembering Scripture allowed the rhetorical structures of his sermons to rise and fall with the text, finding harmony in the tensions, like a great jazz musician whose skill at improvisation is a consequence of hours upon hours of practicing the simple scales. His speech, reflecting the narrative nature of Scripture itself, was as fresh and its forms as novel and fluid as the freedom of sunshine, wind, and rain.

All of this begins with the preacher committing to putting the Bible to memory. Dr. Brown was fond of saying that "before we work on the Bible, we want the Bible to work on us." The mystery of Scripture is that it reads us. We open up the Bible, lay it in front of our lives,

5 Amos Wilder, *Early Christian Rhetoric* (Cambridge: Harvard University Press, 1964),16.

6 See Walter Ong, *Orality and Literacy: The Technologizing of the Word* (London: Meutheon, 1982), 65: "Even in cultures which know and depend on writing but retain a living contact with pristine orality, that is, retain high oral residue, ritual utterance itself is often not typically verbatim. 'Do this in memory of me' Jesus said at the Last Supper (Luke 22:19). Christians celebrate the Eucharist as their central act of worship because of Jesus' directive. But the crucial words that Christians repeat as Jesus' words in fulfilling this directive (that is, the words 'This is my body...' this is the cup of my blood...') do not appear in exactly the same way in any two places where they are cited in the New Testament. The early Christian Church remembered, in pretextual, oral form even in her textualized rituals, and even at those very points where she was command to remember most assiduously."

and discover that we have been laid open to it. This begins with the discipline of putting in the time to interiorize the Scripture we are preaching from week to week. It takes time, but in the long run it saves the preacher time. Because once the Scripture is inside of the preacher, you can keep replaying it again, retrieving its wisdom as needed. Internalizing—or *remembering*—Scripture is the weekly habit of *The Project.* The preacher wants to press the Scripture into their memory, like the best music pressed into vinyl, so that it can be heard again and again. The goal of remembering Scripture is not simply to rehearse lines like an actor performing in a play, but rather to internalize the text so that its meaning begins to perform inside our minds, hearts, and actions. The preacher wants to *see* the text in the mind and *feel* it in the soul, not just study it in order to analyze and critique. When we spend time internalizing the Word so that it can be remembered, it is like a match that ignites the pastoral imagination. This burning imagination allows a sermon to burn with a bright intensity that overcomes the darkness.

The Project aspires to remember not only the biblical story, but also the particular stories of the people and communities who listen to the sermon. Dr. Brown worked to remember the storied lives of those in the pews, speaking their names and remembering their significant moments, and then pulling them into the dialogue with the biblical text, allowing the congregation to hear how God's story intersects with their own. Therefore, a sermon inspired by *The Project* aims to internalize and rehearse through memory both the biblical story and the stories of God's people and bring them together in the sermon to create a shared experience, where our story is pulled into the larger drama of the story of God. In the process, it reorients our perspective of reality to one that participates in a divine history.

The Project, however, remembers so that the sermon can be experienced as a living word that unites head and body, member to member, story within story, living, where the dead come back to life, where flesh is put back on dry bones, where those who were lost are now found. The power of memory is one of the ways that the preacher helps the church practice resurrection for the life of the world. In this experience, we find that the sermon is a place where God's memory allows people to experience the eternal *amen* of the gospel, as the good word that was in the preacher gets into them as well. In this way, the conversation that begins in prayer and moves forward by memory continues as prayer and praise and preaching.

O is for Orality

The O in *Project* is for orality. The sermon that begins on the knees continues with a learning by heart to speak to the ear.

Orality is a commitment to the principles and dynamics of spoken or verbal communication. Preaching is a vocation of the voice. It is in the pulpit that pastors have the mandate to speak of and direct our attention to the God of Israel. This God is first and foremost the God who speaks creation into existence, the God who speaks the consequences of sin in the garden, the God who speaks to Abraham a binding covenant promise, the God who speaks his law to Moses, the God who sends his eternal Word into human flesh to speak a new hope for the world into existence. The biblical God is loquacious. Preaching joins the triune conversation as the preacher finds her voice. Thus, the sermon is always a reverberation of the God who speaks first. Our speaking is always in the context of the God who speaks. Speaking is a necessary action of preaching.

It is important to make this point, because there is a general sense in some quarters in the church that a commitment to oral proclamation is no longer necessary. Misinterpreting St. Francis's advice to "preach the Gospel at all times, and when necessary use words," many become suspicious that preaching is a form of clerical vanity that displaces the "real" action of ministry. Interestingly, there is no evidence that St. Francis, who founded an order of preachers, actually said this. It's a well-intended sentiment, but it has been used to suggest that preaching is not really necessary as long as we live out our faith. Of course, we must live out our faith and embody what we preach. That point is not to be questioned. But if we are not willing to share our faith in speech, then how will anyone know what that faith is? In preaching, acting and speaking come together in the harmony of love and in the power of the Spirit. In this way, preaching is essential for faith.

If *The Project* had a mandatory tattoo, it would be Romans 10:17. This verse should be written as a seal on the forehead of every preacher and engraved on every pulpit: "So faith comes from what is heard, and what is heard comes through the word of Christ." Here, Paul makes it clear that a justifying faith comes from those who have heard. This is why a focus on orality is critical to gospel preaching.

Faith comes from what is heard! This is why *The Project* takes the oral dynamics and properties of orality seriously on behalf of the people of God. The sermon is an event of speech. Preaching is an exercise for the ear, not the eye. This basic and most fundamental point is often lost in a world shaped by print media. Generations of preachers have been trained to write first, to process ideas and organize them in such a way that it fits a logical and coherent sequence for a written essay. Coherence, order, and logic is good and necessary. But preaching is a different activity than essay writing. Hearing is a different activity than reading. Which is why the dynamics of orality are critical for the preacher to take seriously in the pulpit. No one is going to read the sermon that you give; they are going to hear it![7] Orality is reflective of the God who speaks, but it is motivated also by a desire for people to hear. Speaking is in service of hearing.[8]

When I was in seminary, I had an internship with Hope College Campus Ministries. I had prepared my sermon, written it out, and worked hard to internalize it so that I could preach it without notes. Dr. Brown came to Dimnent Chapel to cheer me on. He talked to me before the service. He asked me, "how are you feeling?" I told him that I felt nervous, that I wanted to preach it without notes, but that I was hesitant, because I didn't want to mess up. That is, I wanted to get each word right! He asked if he could look at my sermon. I handed over my manuscript to him. He looked it over, looked at me, and looked again at the pages. Then he tore it in half. "Go preach" he said. I stood stunned. Then he smiled and said again, "Go preach it! It's in you. Trust the Word." With my sermon torn in half, I didn't have time to panic. I had to collect myself and in a few minutes stand before a listening audience and preach what I had prepared. I don't remember the details of the sermon. But I do remember preaching with a sense of freedom I had not had before. Dr. Brown was right. The Word was in me. The sermon was inside my blood stream. I was free because instead of being tied to a piece of paper, I was connected to the people. I had to be totally present in the moment, speaking, interpreting, and communicating to the people orally, rather than fussing about getting the exact word correct from a piece of paper.

This was an important lesson in my education and journey as a preacher. Dr. Brown did not tear up my sermon. Rather, he tore up what I wrote for the sermon. There is a difference. The sermon could not be torn up, because the sermon is always what is spoken aloud, orally, in the moment, with the sound waves traveling through a shared space to enter the ear and transform the heart. The sermon manuscript

7 For a good argument on the writing a sermon for the ear over the eye, see G. Robert Jacks, *Just Say the Word: Writing for the Ear* (Grand Rapids, MI: Eerdmans, 1996).

8 See Walter Ong, *Orality and Literacy*.

is merely a record of thoughts, like minutes from a meeting. What Dr. Brown taught me in that moment is that a commitment to orality gives one a different kind of presence to people, and when speaking to an audience, presence counts as much as precision.

Would any of us go to a dinner party and bring written notes to have a conversation at the table? Or would you go into family gathering with only prepared remarks? Of course not! It would ruin the conversation. How often has the preacher gone into the pulpit and begun to preach, but has lost a sense of connection to those they are speaking to because they are tied to a piece of paper?

The bottom line is that God uses the voice of one person so that we might together hear God's Word. Our voices and words are what God uses to create new realities in the soul and structures of society. When the Word is spoken, it pushes us out of presumed worlds most of us are trapped in and desperately want to flee. It is our words, when spoken and heard with the freedom of the Spirit, that unlock our caged imaginations so that we can see and enter into the expansive geography of God's grace. The preacher is a keeper of words because it is the nature of language to form us, rather than simply inform.[9] This is what the preacher aims for when we begin on our knees, get the word in us and let it come out of the mouth—we keep language personal and intimate in order to make new relationships with God and each other through an encounter of revelation that forms. For when this happens, God speaks his eternal Word, who in the free power of the Holy Spirit echoes down the canyons of time to meet us in our time and place, so that we might be set free by the cadences of the Creator.

J is for Jesus

The J in *Project* is for Jesus. The sermon that begins on the knees continues with a learning by heart to speak to the ear as a witness to Jesus the Christ.

The center of *The Project* is Jesus. Keeping Jesus at the center of the sermon is to proclaim the mystery of the life, death, resurrection, and ascension of Jesus as testified in Holy Scripture. This protects the preacher from being preoccupied with themselves, falling into the temptation to preach what is most pressing on the news cycle, slipping into a moralistic self-help platitude, or believing that our salvation starts and ends with us. To keep Jesus at the center of the sermon is to

9 See Eugene Peterson, *Eat This Book* (Grand Rapids, MI: Eerdmans, 2006), 3.

keep the sermon in the frame of God's mystery in the place where all the riches and treasures of heaven are found.

This was pressed upon me once when a guest preacher came to visit WTS when I was a senior in seminary. I remember being impressed by the rhetorical precision and human insight of the sermon. But at the same time, there was something missing. After the sermon, I went to talk to Dr. Brown to process the dissonance I felt. I asked him what he thought of the sermon that morning. I remember him looking down, then looking me in the eye as he said, "I thought it was a disappointment. Not once was the name of Jesus mentioned." Then he said something I never forgot. "Jesus is on every page and in every verse of the Bible. If you can't find him, then you shouldn't be preaching." For Dr. Brown, what mattered most was that Jesus' name would be exalted above all others. Preaching was in service to the witness of Jesus Christ.

What Dr. Brown preached and taught us to preach in each sermon was an encounter with the crucified and living Jesus Christ. His prayer was that in every sermon Jesus would walk out of the Bible and into the hearts, minds, and actions of those who listen. Jesus is preached not as a mythic figure, a metaphor, or a moral exemplar, but rather as the divine man who lived in time, was crucified, resurrected, and ascended to the right hand of the Father. *The Project* focuses on the person of Jesus because Jesus is the focus of our salvation. He alone is the evangel, the subject and object of the good news, whose revelation overwhelms the world and who shatters our perceived realities.

Jesus is the center of *The Project* because the Bible insists that Jesus is the revelation of God, and therefore the only way to know the living God. The Gospel of John says, "No one has ever seen God. It is God, the only Son [Jesus], ...who has made him known" (John 1:18). The particular and unique claim of the historic Christian faith is that there is no knowledge of God without encountering God's own self-revelation to the world in Jesus Christ. This is why Jesus' own words are so arresting when he says, "The Father and I are one" (John 10:30). Jesus and the Father are one and the same, sharing a life and a symbiotic relationship that cannot be divided, confused, or set against each other. Jesus is the truth of God who directs our one wild life to the one wild God.

This christological focus seeks to keep preaching from becoming a gnostic exercise, in which the sermon is always mentally escaping this world, through affirming the mystery that "the Word became flesh and lived among us" (John 1:14). To make Jesus the center of *The Project* is to keep our focus on this world, because the witness of Jesus is God coming down to us, for us, as one of us. In short, God takes this world seriously by taking the time to put on flesh and dwell as one of us in Christ. Thus, our preaching will at the same time take our lives, our places, and our humanity seriously precisely because in the Father does in the Son. No sermon should ever ignore the human dimension, for to do so would be to lose Jesus as the center of gospel proclamation. As Karl Barth writes in *The Preaching of the Gospel,* "The preacher must not be a visionary, soaring into an unreal world, though his mind may be, no doubt, full of good intentions and noble ideas. Faithful preaching is not visionary, for Holy Scripture was shaped in a very real world."[10]

Jesus as the center also allows us to preach with hope towards a future end. In the end, the Christian hope is that Jesus is going to make all things new (Revelation 21:5). This hope is what allows a preacher the confidence and conviction to offer Jesus to people in their particular circumstances of difficulty, suffering, and even death. Christ keeps our hope alive, and it is hope that allows our faith to find purpose. With Jesus, the future is not defined by our particular constraints but by God's power in the resurrected Christ to bring about new life—to put flesh back on dry bones. This gives preaching a measure of hopefulness that is impossible if Jesus is not the center of the sermon and the omega of history.

Focusing on Jesus as the subject of the sermon keeps God's agency at the center of the gospel. In a culture shaped and defined by individualism, best-practice pragmatism, and market-driven efficiencies, it is easy for preachers to slip into thinking that a sermon's effectiveness, and even others' salvation, falls on their shoulders. There is a temptation in ministry for pastors to want to be the savior rather than point us to the God who saves. Maintaining Jesus at the center of our preaching helps us avoid this temptation by keeping Christ's work the primary agency for our justification and sanctification before God.[11]

10 Karl Barth, *The Preaching of the Gospel* (Philadelphia: Westminster Press, 1963), 48.

11 See for, example, James Torrance, *Worship, Community, and the Triune God of Grace* (Downers Grove, IL: InterVarsity Press, 1996), 65. Here we are reminded that the language of mediation and the role of High Priest brings together the mystery that Jesus is both the one we preach about and the one who preaches, the one we point to, and the one who testifies, the one who justifies, as well as the one who sanctifies: "It is supremely in Jesus Christ that we see the double meaning of grace. Grace means that God gives himself to us as God, freely and unconditionally, to be worshipped and adored. But grace also means that God comes to us in Jesus Christ as man, to do for us and in us what we cannot do. He offers a life of perfect

In Christ, all things, including our salvation and our ongoing lives as disciples, hold together without collapsing back on themselves. When we preach Jesus Christ as the one Lord and savior of the world, the governing dynamics of grace keep together what we often are tempted to split apart and try and do for ourselves. In the end, the habit of recognizing that Jesus is the living center of and the active agent of the sermon means that preachers are freed from a messiah complex. Keeping Jesus at the center suggests that our goal is for the preacher to disappear behind the identity of Jesus. This is what Andrew Purves describes as the "crucifixion of ministry."[12] This kind of sacrificial identity develops and grows as we seek to keep Jesus at the center of *The Project.*

E is for Exegesis

The E in *Project* is for exegesis. The sermon that begins on the knees continues with a learning by heart to speak to the ear as a witness to Jesus the Christ through exegesis of holy Scripture.

Dr. Brown was fond of saying before opening Scripture that "The Bible is the book we love." For him, preaching was merely an extension of his passion to not merely learn, study, or preach Scripture but to assimilate it into his life until it nourished his vision and acts of love, service and fellowship, mission and evangelism for others in Jesus' name. At the heart of this assimilation was a deep commitment to interpreting Scripture so that its many gifts would be shared with as many people as possible. He showed me how to be committed to Scripture, to *eat it,* as Eugene Peterson encourages, by making Scripture part of the daily diet of life.[13]

Dr. Brown always had with him his Bible, and more often than not his Greek New Testament, which he could read from sight. *The Project,* as a set of habits and deep commitments, is animated by a deep love of the written Word that believes each book, each chapter,

---

obedience and worship and prayer to the Father, that we might be drawn by the Spirit in communion with the Father, 'through Jesus Christ our Lord.'"

12 See Andrew Purves, *The Crucifixion of Ministry: Surrendering our Ambitions to the Service of Christ* (Downers Grove, IL: InterVarsity Press, 2007), iii. Here Purves argues that there is nothing redemptive about our ministries, only the ministry of Jesus is redemptive: "Our people don't need us; they need Jesus. Our job is to bear witness to him, trusting that he continues to be the One who forgives, blesses, heals, renews, instructs and brings life out of death." This is what is meant by the "crucifixion of ministry."

13 Peterson, *Eat This Book*, 18.

and each verse of Scripture is a bush that burns but cannot be consumed. We cannot exhaust the meaning of the Bible, which requires constant interpretation of its significance for our lives. This work of interpretation is an ongoing, life-long feast in which the preacher eats Scripture in order to live by faith. There is no serious preaching without first a serious commitment to the exegesis of Scripture.

This is why preachers committed to exegesis value classical training, where the exposure and learning of biblical languages, along with studying the history of interpretation and theological tradition, are invaluable tools in the work of Christian proclamation. These tools alone do not make one a master builder or preacher, but without the tools in hand, it is difficult to construct a sermon with integrity and beauty worthy of a second listen. Exegesis of Scripture is to preaching what air in the lungs is to cycling or running—essential for any sustained movement. As Scripture itself says, "All Scripture is inspired by God and is useful for teaching, for reproof, for correction, and for training in righteousness, so that everyone who belongs to God may be proficient, equipped for every good work" (2 Timothy 3:16).

In preaching courses, I remember Dr. Brown drilling into me, "preach the text!" He was passionate about making the biblical text—not personal experience, worldly knowledge or insight, or the controversy of the day—the primary source of the sermon. To be a preacher means a commitment to being a servant of the Word, and a servant has to serve it, not be served by it. This is why Dr. Brown rarely preached thematic sermons about a particular issue. His commitment to exegetical preaching meant that the sermon was always led by the Bible's vision of God. Such a dedication to exegetical preaching allows the preacher to be given "spectacles" so that she can see and interpret God clearly, and in that light also see and interpret the nature of ourselves, other people, and our place with truer vision.[14]

The work of exegesis is at the same time a work to interpret the people who will listen to the sermon. Dr. Brown was a master of understanding not only what the Bible said, but how to share so that it could be heard by others. That meant that he had to also

[14] See John Calvin, *Institutes of the Christian Religion,* trans. Henry Beveridge (Grand Rapids: Eerdmans, 1953), I.xiv.1. Calvin writes, "Just as old or bleary-eyed men and those with vision, if you thrust before them a most beautiful volume, even if they recognize it to be some sort of writing, yet can scarcely construe two words, but with the *aid of spectacles* will begin to read distinctly; so Scripture, gathering up the otherwise confused knowledge of God in our minds, having dispersed our dullness, clearly shows us the true God."

interpret the people he preached to. Exegetical preaching asks for an emotional intelligence that can communicate the truth of the Bible, by understanding the deep longings, fears, anxieties, loves, and hopes of people. Dr. Brown would often call this "preaching to people's pain." He was able to understand and name where people hurt and how to bring gospel truth to them for healing.

The preacher has to exegete people and their pain as well as Scripture. This kind emotional intelligence is critical to Christian preaching. Self-deception is the easiest temptation to follow in the Christian life, and no preacher, no matter their proficiency or skill, is immune. The knowledge of self that we glean from lenses of exegeting Scripture is that we are prone to sin and yet we are also objects of God's divine grace—loved, forgiven, healed and restored to communion with God through Jesus Christ. Good exegesis holds together the mystery that we are both sinner and saints at the same time. The preacher's job is to interpret our lives so that our desperate need for God is laid bare before the cross and resurrection of Christ.

The Project is a call to exegete not only Scripture, but also the way people feel, think, and imagine their lives, so that our desperate need for Christ may find its way into a living faith. Dr. Brown taught me how to interpret people's stories and then help them interpret their lives in the context of God's story. Interpretation, then, is the work of participating in God's ongoing drama of salvation in the world right now. We help to interpret lives within the very life of God. This means we also have to have a keen sense of how people are tied to and shaped by their place, or culture.

There is no exegeting Scripture in a vacuum. Our interpretation of Scripture is impacted by the place and culture in which we do the work of interpretation. All exegesis is influenced by the culture in which we live. This means that exegetical preaching requires the work of a cultural anthropologist. One has to understand not only what the Bible says but also what it might mean to the people it is shared with. The place where God calls the preacher is at the same time the place where God does his redeeming work in the lives of people. But that place needs to be understood. Exegesis of the Bible requires at the same time an exegesis of our place.

When he was preaching, Dr. Brown always took people's places seriously. His sermons would include the names of local streets or institutions, and he would give the historical meanings their places as well. His sermons would honor their stories, and in the telling of their stories bring them into the larger story of God. He knew that one of the cardinal sins of a pastor is to look down upon or condescend to another's place. If preachers withhold themselves from their place, they are withholding themselves not only from the people of that place but also from God. For there is no place that does not belong to God. The preacher's task is to honor place and give it significance by interpreting it within the context of each sermon.

It is the task of the preacher to exegete the meaning of one's place as a context for God's active grace, in relationship to the interpretation of Scripture and of God's people. But this work of exegesis—of Scripture, people, and place—requires a discipline that is not unlike that of a detective, whose cool reason and observation is what sparks the fresh imaginative insight of truth. It is this truth of Scripture, people, and place that the preacher seeks in every sermon.

C is for Conversion

The C in *Project* is for conversion. The sermon that begins on the knees continues with a learning by heart to speak to the ear as a witness to Jesus the Christ through exegesis of the book we love with the hope that all hearts will be converted back to God's love.

If the sermon's aim is to help the hearer to encounter the person of Jesus Christ, then the prayer is that in this encounter Christ will not only meet us where we are but will also love us enough not to leave us there. The Christian faith hinges on God's work in Christ, and his work creates the power for our transformation in him. This transformation comes from a faith that follows repentance, a turning around of our lives to follow Christ's narrow way.

"Conversion" is one way to describe this mysterious transformation. It is a recognition that the only way to participate in God's saving life is to trust our heart, mind, soul and strength to the God of Israel. Whether sudden or protracted, the Christian faith requires conversation.

Dr. Brown made conversion a part of his preaching ministry, because he was someone who experienced the power of conversion himself. He knew firsthand that it is possible for God to make anyone "a new creation" in Christ, because that was his own story. While on spring break in 1971, at Daytona, Florida, a fuzzy-headed Tim Brown, stumbled upon a band playing music. He stopped to listen to the music, and then the leader of the band began to preach from 2 Corinthians 5:17: "So if anyone is in Christ, there is a new creation: everything old has passed away; see, everything has become new!" The preacher invited anyone to give their life over to God—to start fresh be made a new creation in Christ. It was in that moment that the young Tim Brown heard the call of God. He felt the warming power and irresistible pull to believe in the good news of Jesus Christ. He was converted. He was a new creation as a Christian.

This sense that God can change someone's life suddenly, dramatically, through a simple message, never left Dr. Brown. It was always at the surface, the hope that this may be that moment for someone listening to him, and so no moment could be wasted. It was not that every sermon had an altar call or an invitation to sit on "the anxious bench"; it didn't. But each sermon Dr. Brown offered had the feel of an invitation from God, calling you back to him and promising a fresh start, and all you needed to do was to turn around in good faith and come home to a loving God. It was that simple.

Conversion, however, was never a ploy or a manipulation in Dr. Brown's preaching. He always maintained that this was the jurisdiction of God. Only the God who makes the heart can change the heart. Conversion by any other means is merely coercion. In other words, conversion is God's gift, not a result of gaming out what rhetorical techniques, psychological insights, or emotional buttons will "work" on people. A personal conversion to Christ is always accomplished by the primary work of the Holy Spirit. It is the Spirit, sent from the Father and the Son, who ignites a faith that transforms us into a new creation. This means preachers cannot manipulate or cajole conversion but can only participate and bear witness to God's primary work through the Spirit.

It is hubris for the preacher to think if she employs a particular style, language, or form, or stages an invitation at the end of a sermon, that she can engineer a conversion. God is free, of course, to use these things, but it needs to be clear that if God uses human efforts for another's conversion, it is God, not the preacher, who is behind it. Conversion in Christ is above all a work of grace, and grace is always the agency of God.

We don't preach for preaching's sake; we preach so that people's lives might be transformed by the power of God so that they might find healing, wholeness, and the peace of God. This power to transform lives comes from the Word of God, not the sermon or the preacher. God's grace, and grace alone, may convert us through his Word. As the apostle Paul affirms, "Faith comes from what is heard, and what is heard comes through the word of Christ" (Romans 10:17).

Dr. Brown preached for gospel conversion, trusting of the Word of God to speak freely. Our salvation is secure in Christ, the eternal Word made flesh, on the cross. It is on Calvary, through the atonement of Jesus Christ, that humanity is reconciled to God, when he takes away the sin of the world. Jesus saved us once for all on the cross, but our participation in that salvation requires daily conversations of the heart and mind, of our wallet, independence, and politics. Dr. Brown was fond of sharing a quote attributed to Martin Luther about there being three conversations in the Christian life: "the conversion of one's heart, the conversion of one's mind, and the conversion of one's wallet." Preaching for conversation means that when the Word is offered freely, God may use that moment to confront areas in our lives that we have been holding on to but need to hand over to God. It can be painful. But on the other side of the pain is freedom! This means the preacher is always saying urgently that today is the day to repent—to turn around right now back to God. For in our turning back to God, we find ourselves stepping onto a new path, though narrow, that will lead us back to life, and life abundantly.

Conversion, or *metanoia*, cannot be cajoled, manipulated, engineered, or prescribed. The preacher who preaches for conversion anticipates that something is going to happen, but sometimes it doesn't. Yet we keep preaching in faith. Preaching to convert is an act of trust in God and the power and promise of God's Word. God will do something through the faithful preaching of the gospel. We don't know what, but we expect that God will do something new. The Word shatters our perceived realities and pulls us into a world from which we can never return. Gospel conversation is less a rational persuasion than a consequence of being overwhelmed by God's transcendence. The hope of any preacher is for God to use our sermons to reveal this transcendent reality by pulling the hearer so far into the narrative Word, into that "thin place" where heaven and earth meet, that God's transcendent breath becomes the very air they breathe. In other words, *The Project* claims that conversion is less about offering information about God than about finding oneself participating in the reality of God. Hence, when to comes to conversation, *The Project* takes to heart the old proverb credited to Antoine de Saint-Exupéry: "If you want to build a ship, don't drum up the men to gather wood, divide the work, and give orders. Instead, teach them to yearn for the vast and endless sea."

T is for Tradition

The T in *Project* is for tradition. The sermon that begins on the knees continues with a learning by heart to speak to the ear as a witness to Jesus the Christ through exegesis of the book we love for conversion to enter and extend the tradition of Christian faith. This tradition of faith is one that seeks to be renewed by continued understanding through learning.

One of the primary lessons I learned from Dr. Brown was the importance of submitting to the hard work of learning a Christian tradition. He taught me that tradition, at its best, is meant to be a servant, not a master. That is, a preacher must have a teachable heart, always learning from the best scholars and poets, theologians and pastors, leaders and artists of Christian history. Dr. Brown was always reading and learning something new. He had what you might describe as a "growth mindset." Nearly every sermon he preached was supported or illustrated by a quote from a great Christian thinker, an allusion to history, or a reference to a book. This showed me that a sermon can look outside of a preacher's own personal experience for relevance, and at the same time it pointed me to a larger vicarious experience in the body of Christ. Dr. Brown absorbed a Christian tradition of the past in such a way that he could make it resound back to us as a fresh word for today. Dr. Brown was a preacher who was shaped by a larger conversation, and he invited me to join in that dialogue.

But to do that, I had to learn the tradition first. Dr. Brown often did this through the ministry of books. In his study was a wall of old and used volumes of books, and each one was read, highlighted, dog-eared, and bruised from use. He would often pass onto me old copies of Augustine, Calvin, Theresa, Lewis, Forsyth, or Spurgeon. After nearly every meeting with Dr. Brown, I would leave his office if not with a new book in hand to read, then a title of a recommended book I needed to go check out from the library. My awareness of a larger intellectual tradition grew because I had a teacher who was committed to introducing me to the giants who went before, the giants upon whose shoulders we all stand. But he did not merely just introduce me to authors and books titles. He showed me how to integrate their wisdom into daily life. Dr. Brown expected me to read in such a way that I would absorb a particular kind of conversation, a historic way of thinking, which one day I would contribute to in my own voice. For Dr. Brown, sharing the tradition meant passing on the best wisdom of the church from one generation to the next.

Dr. Brown exposed me to the reality that a preacher's job is to participate in an old tradition, stretching as far back as the patriarchs and prophets. Our tradition of learning includes Mosses and David, Isaiah and Jeremiah, Ruth and Esther, Paul and John, Ignatius and Theresa, Calvin and Pascal, Eugene Peterson and Martin Luther King Jr., and thousands upon thousands of other faithful voices we have never heard before. Dr. Brown gave me a history that had a through line that reached to me. This made me aware that I was part of something large and long, and that I wasn't alone and thrown back upon myself to figure out what it meant to be in ministry. In this sense, what Dr. Brown taught me was that tradition *is* the teacher.

For some, this emphasis on learning a tradition for ministry may sound counter-cultural. Within our cultural moment, old ways are often forgotten, or worse, ignored in favor of the next fad or fashion of the day. In some Christian circles, there is an assumption that because the Spirit is always doing something new, whatever is new must therefore be from the Spirit of God. *The Project* is a counter-cultural call to avoid this temptation. What Dr. Brown taught me through a respect for a Christian tradition is that the Spirit has always been at work and does not contradict herself, and therefore tradition is a way to understand the Spirit. Tradition offers us the wisdom that, before the living God, "What has been is what will be, and what has been done is what will be done; there is nothing new under the sun" (Ecclesiastes 1:9).

Tradition teaches the preacher that the goal of the sermon is not to seek originality but rather to find harmony and faithful participation in this ancient choir of gospel proclamation. Thus, the old ways often have fresh power in a new day. In the care of the soul, sometimes the freshest insight is discovered in aged and dog-eared wisdom. Traditions such as praying the Psalms, orality, internalizing Scripture, and preaching with an eye to Jesus and gospel conversion, can be experienced not only as relevant but also as innovative. Every generation must claim these traditions for themselves for the renewal of the church.

There is a danger of thinking innovation always needs to replace tradition, instead of seeing tradition as the guide that gives innovation its start. It may even be argued that embracing tradition is the path to innovation. To blindly embrace current cultural assumptions without an honest reflection on the practiced wisdom of the past, is to fall helpless, like chaff in the wind, without the rooted nourishment of the past. This is why G. K. Chesterton once wrote, "Tradition means giving a vote to most obscure of all classes, our ancestors. It is the democracy of the dead."[15]

Which is why *The Project* encourages reading from a deep well, dug by a centuries-long theological conversation that transcends our current cultural moment. To learn a tradition requires disciplined patience. There are no short cuts. The preaching life is demanding. It demands the integrity to read and reflect on primary theological works and trusted practices that form the soul. Tradition asks of us to submit our intellectual, emotional, and spiritual formation to what Eugene Peterson might call a "long obedience in the same direction." This journey is not easy. But for those who are called to this work, it yields benefits, and it produces an abundance of spiritual fruit in not only in pastoral ministry, but for one's life.

Conclusion

I learned *The Project* from Dr. Tim Brown. He was my teacher and my guide into a larger world of Christian ministry. This was a world I always assumed existed but didn't know where to find or how to enter. He gave me the map and the keys to the open the door. For this gift I am forever grateful. His mentoring offered me both encouragement and challenge. What he passed onto me, I want to steward so that I may offer it forward to a new generation. This is the work I have dedicated my life to as the dean of the chapel at Hope College. This brief essay is written with the hope of passing on what I learned from Dr. Brown to those who will preach long after we are gone.

The Project is a way of living as a preacher that is in one sense exclusive, but it is also radically inclusive. It invites all pastors everywhere to join in this work and witness. I invite you to join us. Let this be a moment when we recommit ourselves to the work of Christian preaching. For it is in this work that the renewal not only of the church but of our own faith and vocation may find fresh power and energy for

15 See G. K. Chesterton, *Orthodoxy* (New York: John Lane Co., 1908), 85. This quote by Chesterton is worth sharing in full: "Tradition refuses to submit to the small and arrogant oligarchy of those who merely happen to be walking about. All democrats object to men being disqualified by the accident of birth; tradition objects to their being disqualified by the accident of death. Democracy tells us not to neglect a good man's opinion, even if he is our groom; tradition asks us not to neglect a good man's opinion, even if he is our father."

the unknown future. For there has never been a better time to preach the good news of Jesus Christ! Amen.

CHAPTER 8

"God's Powerful Instrument: The Triume God's Action Through Scripture"

J. Todd Billings

Dr. Timothy Brown has been known for decades for his love of preaching, emerging from a loving trust in Scripture, which he internalizes, dwells upon, and proclaims. This essay explores how the Triune God of Scripture is not simply proclaimed in such preaching but is the central actor in the sending forth of the Word to his people. It is God's chosen instrument of self-presentation, through the Spirit, in Christ, given to comfort, rebuke, and feed the beloved children of the Father. In other words, Scripture is not our tool for our purposes (e.g., self-help or worldly prosperity). Scripture is the Triune God's tool to be used for his own purposes. As receivers of the Word in Christ, we enter into God's work as we dwell in Scripture, and we are empowered by the Spirit to grow into our true identity: children of the Father, loving God and neighbor, bearing witness to Christ and his kingdom in a confused and darkened world.

This essay is a revised version of a section in my book *The Word of God for the People of God.*[1] It explores how we might move beyond

[1] J. Todd Billings, *The Word of God for the People of God* (Grand Rapids, MI: Eerdmans, 2010).

viewing Scripture as merely presenting a set of abstract truths. Instead, the word of God in Scripture is tied into the Triune drama of God's redeeming action, calling us out from "lesser dramas" that we are so often tempted to inhabit. This revised excerpt is reprinted by permission of the publisher. Parts have been deleted for the sake of space, and some additions have been added to enhance the argument and flow of the modified essay.

✞

When the word of God in Scripture comes to the people of God through the Spirit, it does not simply give "information" about God, but mediates the powerful *action* of God. God's speech through Scripture performs very real *actions* through the Spirit—giving life to dry bones, overcoming alienation through fellowship. Herman Bavinck, an early-twentieth-century Christian dogmatician, put it this way: God "is always present in his word" such that the word "is never separate from God, from Christ, from the Holy Spirit."[2] Thus, the word of God *performs actions* in God's own power. "The word that proceeds from the mouth of God is indeed always a power accomplishing that for which God sends it forth."[3]

In and through Scripture, God promises, commands, beckons, and admonishes. All of these actions involve more than just giving "information" about God—even as they are disclosed to us through Scripture. When promising a covenantal relationship to Abram, God says "I will make of you a great nation, and I will bless you" (Genesis 12:2a). God makes *promises* to Abram, and these *promises* extend beyond simply Abram to others included in God's covenant people. Christian readers should not be content with a reading that simply says, "God is the sort of God who makes covenant with Abram and his people." This statement of "information" does not go far enough. The *state of affairs* between God and Abram has changed because of God's words, just as when in a wedding words are spoken to declare that a couple is now "man and wife." God *promises* and *makes covenant* with Abram—it is an action. And if readers see *themselves* as within Abram's covenant, God *promises* and *makes covenant* with the reader by means of the text.

What difference does this make? If all of God's actions of speech are "translated" into simply "true information about God," then

2 Herman Bavinck, *Reformed Dogmatics: Holy Spirit, Church, and New Creation*, vol. 4, trans. John Vriend, ed. John Bolt (Grand Rapids, MI: Baker Academic, 2008), 459.

3 Bavinck, *Reformed Dogmatics*, vol.4, 458.

we respond differently to this biblical text than if God *acts* through his speech. "God is a God who makes promises to Abram and his descendants" keeps God's word at arm's length. "We go to church, and they tell us about God," a parishioner might think. "It is reassuring to know that God is the kind of God who makes promises to people—that's good, because I think it's good to make promises." But if, through the action of God's speech, God changes the state of affairs—God *makes promises* to us—then we must consider how to respond. How am I to see my life, my marriage, or my workplace in light of the fact that the God of Israel makes promises to me and my faith community? How am I to live now, as one whom God actively "blesses" and promises that "in you all the families of the earth shall be blessed" (Gen. 12:2-3b)? How do my actions toward other "peoples," nations, and cultures live into God's promise or deny it? God *promises*, God *blesses*, and in the midst of this, God *calls* us to participate in his action of blessing the peoples of the earth.

Moving from a one-dimensional to a three-dimensional reception of God's word is part of entering into the Spirit's work of being renewed in Christ. In Matthew's gospel, Jesus tells the parable of the sower to talk about the various responses to the word of God's kingdom. Jesus quotes Isaiah that some will hear, but never understand, see, but never perceive (Matthew 13:14). But Jesus measures "hearing" and "seeing" through the *response* to the seed of the word—the fertile soil bears fruit and "produces a crop" (Matthew 13:23, NIV). A proper response to God's word is not just about receiving information that is transmitted but perceiving the powerful action of God in that speech and responding by the Spirit. Apart from the Spirit, Jonathan Edwards says, we receive God's word as an abstract word, like reading a dictionary entry about "honey." But through the Spirit, we gain a fuller reception of the word, tasting the sweetness of honey so that we respond to the word with our affections and delight.[4]

Ultimately, Jesus' parable of the sower points to an *inability* to enter into the new state of affairs brought about through God's word, to be the initiating actors in a loving relationship with God. Soil is powerless to change itself. As Marianne Meye Thompson noted in a commencement address at Western Theological Seminary on this

4 Jonathan Edwards, "A Treatise Concerning Religious Affections," in *A Jonathan Edwards Reader*, ed. John E. Smith et al. (New Haven: Yale University Press, 1995), 160–61.

parable, we would like to talk about "purpose-driven soil." But soil is inert, powerless to change itself into another type of soil.[5]

Thus, as readers of Scripture, "we were dead through our trespasses and sins" (Ephesians 2:1). We cannot generate or manipulate the true power of Scripture for our own purposes. However, thankfully, while dead in our trespasses, God "made us alive together with Christ." (Ephesians 2:5). For while we taste the eschatological reality of life in Christ, we still struggle with the deadening effect of sin. In our sin, we still often hear God's word through Scripture in a way that is one-dimensional—an abstract, mildly interesting word about God. In our sin, we do not receive it as a word that announces a new state of affairs, implicating our lives and action through God's promising, asking, electing, and commanding action. Yet, since Christians are united to the true, active humanity of Christ, reading Scripture "in Christ" will always be an active affair. When we read Scripture, we do so as ones who have been made alive by the Spirit with Christ himself, the one in whom Triune God dwells in fullness. Thus, when we read Scripture in Christ, the Spirit empowers us to enter into the triune drama and show the Spirit's own fruit in response to the word. The translation of God's word in Scripture into abstract "information" is not just bad hermeneutics. It is a sinful refusal to participate in the active life of union with Christ.

Acting in Lesser Dramas: Reading Practices Which (Unintentionally) Tell Lesser Stories than the Gospel

Before examining reading practices that participate in the triune drama of salvation, we should consider for a few moments some of the "temptations" that need to be overcome in reading Scripture. The temptations are legion, but because we are dealing in an area of practical wisdom, specific examples can help sharpen our thinking for situations we are yet to encounter. These examples focus on how Scripture is preached and taught, but they apply as well to the ways in which Christians approach Scripture in other contexts.

Temptation #1: *In order to make Scripture "relevant," we make ourselves the primary focus of scriptural interpretation, dislocating the centrality of the Triune God and his saving work.* If we assume that teaching or preaching about God will seem "irrelevant" to a congregation, it is tempting to change the subject to a source of endless fascination: the hearers

[5] Commencement address, "At Four-to-One Odds, Why Take Up Sowing?" Western Theological Seminary, Holland, MI, May 14, 2007.

themselves. The hearers are concerned with how to pay the bills, how to fit in at school, how to have a better marriage. God will take care of God. Why not focus directly upon ourselves in teaching and preaching Scripture?

For example, one pastor decided to preach a sermon addressing a question that everyone faces: "how to deal with criticism." Guided by this question, he chose to preach on Romans 8:1-4, beginning with "There is therefore now no condemnation for those who are in Christ Jesus" and continuing on with "the law of the Spirit" with "the law of sin and death." We are called to walk according to the Spirit, which means we should reject the legalistic demands of others when they criticize us. We should be like Paul, who, grounded in his acceptance from God (from whom there is "no condemnation"), was empowered to listen to legitimate criticism and to ignore condemning, legalistic criticism. The preacher mentioned Christ and the Spirit only in passing, because the real *point* of his interpretation was to glean advice about how we should deal with criticism.

In using this text to set up Paul as a model for "how to deal with criticism," the pastor obscured the subject matter (*sache*) of the text—the significance of God's action in Jesus Christ and the Holy Spirit, the subject which animates Paul's text. The pastor assumed that such a message is "abstract" and therefore not essential in forming the actual content of his message. However, the pastor could probably have reached his same practical insights by preaching on a selection from Greek mythology, or any other number of texts. The "practical" insights he desired were nearly oblivious to the divine drama mediated by the biblical text.

The scandalous part of this approach is that it fails to realize that leading hearers to see and experience the triune drama of salvation through the biblical text is one of the most "practical" things a teacher or preacher can do. Stated bluntly, to preach or teach about the Triune God's action in the world *is* to preach about the practical lives of Christians. Why? Because believers are filled with the Holy Spirit and are being transformed into Christ's image, empowered to live in gratitude to the Father. This is "good news" for all parts of life—for Christians struggling with criticism, with finances, with family trouble, with suffering and injustice in a broken world. When read with a hermeneutic of a trinitarian theology of salvation, Scripture becomes a practical book for discerning the saving work of the Trinity in the messiness and ambiguities of life—for Christ is the fulfillment of God's creational and covenantal promises, and our union with the living Christ opens our eyes to the new world of the kingdom.

Temptation #2: *In a desire for "new" or "expert" insights, we reduce the interpretation of Scripture to the conveying of historical information.* Research about the history "behind the biblical text" is an important part of the overall task of interpretation. However, historical reconstruction is never the final "ending point" for a Christian interpretation of Scripture, or for the preaching and teaching of Scripture in the church. The proper interpretive ending point for Christians is for Scripture to nourish love for God and neighbor and deepen our fellowship with God in Christ by the Spirit. Historical reconstruction can be helpful, but it should not be an end in itself. Unfortunately, modern readers often focus far more upon historical background and reconstructions than the realities mediated by the text itself. But when extrabiblical material moves one *away* from engaging the actual text of Scripture rather than *deeper into* such an engagement, preachers and teachers begin to tell a lesser story than the gospel of the Triune God's saving work in the world.

For example, I recall a sermon in which the minister sought to use "behind-the-text history" to give a fresh reading of Jesus' conversation with the two thieves on the cross in Luke 23:39-43. Although Luke's text simply refers to the other two men being crucified as "criminals," the minister said that some commentators believe that these criminals were probably "Zealots," members of a revolutionary Jewish group violently protesting Roman rule. The sermon then proceeded to focus upon giving a historical account of the rise of the Zealots and to speculate about how one might draw lessons from the experience of the Zealots and their effort to overthrow Roman rule. Rather than use historical inquiry to bring insight into the Lukan text, the biblical text became a stepping stone for portraying a history behind the text, which became the real subject matter from which the imperatives of the sermon were drawn.

In an effort to give a "fresh" reading of the text, the sermon obscured the narrative that the Lukan text was telling. The sermon itself became wholly contingent upon an extrabiblical judgment that "the criminals were 'probably' Zealots." Some commentators claim this, but others claim that the criminals were not Zealots. Instead of respecting the narrative within the text (and using extrabiblical information to move deeper into that text) the sermon ended up focusing upon historical information as an end in itself. Then it drew applications from its own reconstructed history. Yet the biblical text is not just one among many sources for reconstructing a story that then functions as a means of grace. The word of God comes *through* the biblical text. Reading Scripture is about discerning a mystery—the mystery of the Triune God. It should not be reduced to conveying historical information from which we draw our application.

Participating in the Drama I: Reading Scripture as a Spiritual Discipline

For Christians, Scripture is not the sort of book we should simply skim or "read for content." The *way* we read it matters. Scripture is a gift given in loving fellowship, and our way of reading should be fitting for this gift. The psalmist writes, "I treasure your word in my heart...O Lord; teach me your statutes. With my lips I declare all the ordinances of your mouth. I delight in the way of your decrees as much as in all riches. I will meditate on your precepts, and fix my eyes on your ways. I will delight in your statutes; I will not forget your word" (Psalm 119:11-16). For the people of God, the words of Scripture are life-giving words to be treasured, delighted in, meditated upon, proclaimed, and remembered. They require attention—the attention of fixing our eyes on the word and work of God, the attention of delighting and remembering God's word both "day and night" (Psalm 1:2).

In the New Testament, we continue to see that Scripture is to be remembered and chewed on rather than skimmed. When tempted by Satan, Jesus responds with Scripture that he has memorized (Matthew 4:1-11). When Ephesians says to "be strong in the Lord and in the strength of his power," we are told that "the word of God" is "the sword of the Spirit." (Ephesians 6:10, 17). The book of Colossians admonishes believers to "let the word of Christ dwell in you richly" —not just "know what the word of Christ says" but let it "dwell in you" (Colossians 3:16). The Gospel of John shows the trinitarian dynamic of this "dwelling," for the Spirit sent to believers will "glorify" Christ, and "will take what is mine and declare it to you" (John 16:14). Together with the Old Testament, the New Testament affirms that Scripture is to be chewed on, delighted in, wrestled with, and meditated upon day and night. As the *Book of Common Prayer* states, we should pray to "hear" the holy Scriptures, and we should "read, mark, learn, and inwardly digest them."[6] We are called to feed upon Scripture, to allow Scripture to

6 *The Book of Common Prayer* (New York: Church Hymnal Corp., 1979), 184.

dwell in us. And for Christians, this practice has a trinitarian shape—such that if we belong to Jesus Christ, God's word in Christ dwells in us through the Spirit's mediation. "Knowing Scripture" for the Christian is a matter of spiritual survival, a matter of participating in the Spirit's new creation in Christ.

Ultimately, why do we "meditate" on Scripture in a way that is different from other books? Because as God's chosen means for communicating his triune presence, the scriptural canon is different from any other book. In a canonical account of reading, "things to be read" are "divided into two basic categories: the canon, the reading of which is essential and primary; and everything else. The Canon is deep and inexhaustible; everything else, while useful, is shallow and can be used up. Everything noncanonical (nonscriptural) is to be read in the light of what is canonical."[7] The Christian canon is in a different category from other books—and requires different ways of reading than do other books—as an "inexhaustible" fountain delivering God's transformative grace in Christ.

Because of the inexhaustible richness of the scriptural canon, Christians in the past have "fed upon" Scripture by combining meditation and memorization with prayer. Consider the words of John Cassian (ca. 360–435), who combines an emphasis upon Scripture memorization with a focused practice of prayer:

> Hence the successive books of the Holy Scripture must be diligently committed to memory and ceaselessly reviewed. This continual meditation will bestow on us double fruit. First, inasmuch as the mind's attention is occupied with reading and with preparing to read, it cannot be taken captive in the entrapments of harmful thoughts. Then, the things that we have not been able to understand because our mind was busy at the time, things that we have gone through repeatedly and are laboring to memorize, we shall see more clearly afterward when we are free from every seductive deed and sight, and especially when we are silently meditating at night.[8]

7 Paul J. Griffiths, "Reading as a Spiritual Discipline," in *The Scope of Our Art*, ed. L. Gregory Jones and Stephanie Paulsell (Grand Rapids, MI: Eerdmans, 2002), 45. Griffiths is summarizing a view exposited by Hugh of St. Victor (1096–1141), but one that has much in common with other premodern approaches to the Christian canon.

8 Qtd. in Richard Lischer, *The Company of Preachers* (Grand Rapids, MI: Eerdmans, 2002), 187.

For all Christians, Scripture memorization and praying with and through Scripture are ways to enter into the Spirit's work—to move one's mind from the head-spinning stream of words around us and to focus upon God's word in Scripture. For Christian preachers and teachers in particular, prayerful memorization and meditation upon Scripture can provide the "space" to hear the particular texture, logic, and flow of a biblical text that God has taken up for his own purposes. Since God uses Scripture as an instrument of grace, memorization is a way to patiently and humbly allow the words of Scripture to be chewed and digested, incorporated into our lives by the Spirit's power.

Ultimately, approaching Scripture with prayerful meditation is not so much an "exegetical method" as a disposition appropriate to Scripture because Scripture is the instrument of God's communicative fellowship. Prayerful meditation is not, in itself, an "argument" for legitimate exegesis. When discussing the exegetical merits of a particular interpretation, it is not sufficient to say "I prayed about it." Christians who pray are still fallible. Christians who pray can still be sloppy and self-deceiving readers. Christians who pray are still sinners. Nevertheless, Scripture is properly approached with a sense that it is God's food, given to us to be "eaten, chewed, gnawed, [and] received in unhurried delight."[9] This is especially valuable in community, as various Christian traditions recognize in the "Daily Office" of prayerful meditation upon Scripture. Without this prayerful and meditative dimension in our reading, Scripture can be quickly reduced to "information, mere tools and data" to be used for our own purposes. In such a case, "we silence the living voice and reduce words to what we can use for convenience and profit."[10] The disposition and practice of prayerful meditation upon Scripture is a way to allow a pause of "silence" before hearing the word of God, a way of seeking to participate in the work of the Spirit, who speaks a word beyond our own scheming and manipulation.

Participating in the Drama II: Scripture and the Ministry of Word and Sacrament

A humble reception and worshipful embrace of God's word is paradigmatic to the identity of the people of God. From God's word to Adam and Eve in the Garden, to God's promise to Abram, to God's

9 Eugene Peterson, *Eat This Book: A Conversation in the Art of Spiritual Reading* (Grand Rapids, MI: Eerdmans, 2006), 11.

10 Peterson, *Eat This Book*, 11.

law given to Israel through Moses, God's word is a fellowship-creating act that calls forth human response. Ultimately, Christians have fellowship with God through the sending of the fellowship-creating Word, "made flesh for us and our salvation," in the words of the Nicene Creed. As a people made one by the Spirit in Christ's body, we gather to celebrate and enact the new life of the Spirit by hearing, touching, tasting, and singing about the mighty acts of the God of Israel made known to us in Christ. Scripture is our precious means for discerning the triune drama of salvation, and in worship we enter into this drama in remembrance, in communion with God and others, and in hope for God's coming new creation.

The sacraments and the proclamation of Scripture are considered "means of grace" by many Christians because of their special role in the economy of salvation: both Word and sacrament hold forth the heart of the gospel through creaturely means (through human proclamation and the elements of water, bread, and wine). The New Testament uses a variety of images to speak about the meaning of baptism, including those of cleansing, new life, and the gift of the Spirit. But one of the most all-encompassing images for this act of initiation into the church is that of "union with Christ."[11] In baptism, a person is united to the death and resurrection of Jesus Christ by the Spirit's power, and baptism then presents a vocation for life-long growth into this identity in Christ, living by the Spirit rather than the flesh (Romans 6:1-14). Just as baptism is an initiation into a life of union with Christ, the Lord's Supper is a participation in Christ, nourishment through communion with Jesus Christ and his body, the church, by the Spirit's power. Both sacraments involve a scripturally mediated remembrance of God's mighty works finding culmination in Christ, communion with God and others through Christ by the Spirit, and hope for the final consummation of God's promises when creatures will celebrate complete communion with God, as the Lamb of God feasts with his bride.

The proclamation of Scripture functions in a similar way as the sacraments as the means by which those who are united to Christ by the Spirit remember, commune, and hope together. Preaching is not the proclamation of a human effort to find God, but the proclamation of the revelatory history that we access through Scripture. Preaching

11 James Brownson, *The Promise of Baptism* (Grand Rapids, MI: Eerdmans, 2007), 54–59.

proclaims the great drama of creation, fall, and redemption. Preaching tells the great story of the way the Triune God incorporates sinners into the divine life through the forgiveness and renewal provided in the incarnation, life, cross, and resurrection of Christ. And preaching does this in a way that enacts the church's own identity—presenting the word of the Living Head to the body of Christ, so that it can grow in its life in the Spirit, in service to the Father. Preaching is, in some sense, "about Scripture," but it must simultaneously be "about Jesus Christ," whose presence animates the worship of Christians through the Spirit's power.

As a result, Christian preaching should approach Scripture as a unified canon held together in its witness and fulfillment in Jesus Christ, not simply as a collection of varied, individual "texts."[12] Seminaries tend to train students to treat Scripture as a set of texts: each scriptural text is understood in its immediate literary and ancient historical context. While these contextual concerns are valuable, preachers need to be very clear about the canonical function of all biblical texts, particularly when it comes to Christian worship: preaching on atomized, individualized texts does not necessarily lead the hearers to focus upon the gospel of Christ and the Spirit's transforming work.[13] In a word, such an approach does not make disciples. In desperation, many pastors try to hold the congregation's attention by offering "flattened, trivialized truth by taking categories of biblical faith and representing them in manageable shapes without the material substance of the Word, Christ himself."[14] When preaching and worship is centered around atomized texts, the congregation does not encounter the Word through the words of Scripture, but "discrete abstract topics packaged and transmitted" in a way that "reduce[s] the mystery of God to problems and solutions" on a self-help level, displacing the need for finding one's identity in

12 This paragraph draws upon Michael Pasquarello III's excellent paper, "Redeeming the Time: Homiletic Theology for a Pilgrim People," Calvin Institute of Christian Worship, January 2008.

13 As Richard Hays writes, while theological exegesis should attend to "the literary wholeness of individual scriptural witnesses" and the distinct voices in the scriptural witness, theological exegesis "can never be content only to describe the theological perspectives of the individual authors; instead, it always presses forward to *the synthetic question of canonical coherence*" which asks "how any particular text fits into the larger biblical story of God's gracious action" ("Reading the Bible with Eyes of Faith: The Practice of Theological Exegesis," in *Sharper Than a Two-Edged Sword: Preaching, Teaching, and Living the Bible,* ed. Michael Root and James J. Buckley [Grand Rapids, MI: Eerdmans, 2008], 91).

14 Pasquarello, "Redeeming the Time," 1.

Christ through the Spirit.[15] Preaching on atomized texts rather than the canon is not preaching the gospel of Jesus Christ.

The centrality of a christological-pneumatological account of the canon applies to the task of Christian formation and education as well. For example, one widely used set of church book-based Bible studies puts "text" over "canon" in this way: "Scripture should be allowed to speak for itself. If the Bible is understood on its own terms, it will convey its own truth. Biblical understanding should be a prelude to theological belief. The Bible should inform theology, not theology the Bible."[16] On the one hand, this account shows some canonical intuitions—it speaks of "Scripture" and "the Bible" as a unified book with a unified witness. But with this admission a problem arises. For Christians, the extremely diverse collection of books and genres in the Bible find their canonical unity only in relation to their witness to Jesus Christ. But that is a claim from "theology"—a claim that the study contends should never precede "biblical understanding." But the question we are to ask is *what kind of "biblical understanding" are we seeking?* Presumably, if one consistently follows the viewpoint indicated by this series, Old Testament texts should *not* be understood in light of Jesus Christ, but exclusively in relation to their historical-literary context. But then we have lost a unified "Scripture," as well as the indispensable sense that the function of all Scripture should be to form believers deeper into Christ's image by the Spirit's power. Christian formation and education need to be clear that they are not simply transmitting "information" or "God's word" in a generic form, but that we seek the Word through the word of God in Scripture.

Why are worship, Christian education, and the overall ministry of the Word and sacrament so important? Ultimately, it is because the gospel of the triune drama of salvation is held forth to us—and to the world—in these acts. Liturgy, preaching, and sacraments all bear worshipful witness to the world-altering reality of the living Christ. All of these ministries should be held together in their purpose and function. In these acts of Christian worship, believers taste the kingdom through their encounter with the living Christ, by means of the life-giving Spirit, who shows us our adopted identity as children of the Father. Worship tells us who we are as the church: the bride of Christ,

15 Pasquarello, "Redeeming the Time," 1–2.

16 "Theological Approach," Kerygma Bible Studies, accessed March 26, 2021, https://kerygma.com/pages/theology.

citizens in a new kingdom. And it forms us deeper and deeper into the gospel—a gospel that's all about Christ and all about the Trinity.

In many ways, the question for pastors, worship leaders, and educators is how to *reorient* the ministries of the church back toward the Triune God of the gospel. This immediately raises other questions about how worship, preaching, and education are organized. A "lectionary" approach can bring a congregation on a journey through the life of Christ in each given year—it can be an excellent way for congregations to grow deeper into their identity as Christ's bride. Another approach, which rose to prominence in the Reformation, is *lectio continua*, in which there is preaching or teaching continuously through a particular book of the Bible. While the *lectio continua* approach has the advantage of encouraging a congregation to move deeply in a particular book of Scripture, it has the disadvantages of not having the canonical variety of passages found in the lectionary, or its structure based around the life of Christ.

Ultimately, congregations can move deeper into acting in the triune drama of God with the lectionary, *lectio continua*, a combination of the two, or another approach for organizing the use of Scripture in worship and education. The key is to use whatever decided-upon approach in a way that is self-consciously canonical and that self-consciously interprets Scripture as a way to discern the mystery of the Word in the words, being transformed through Scripture into our true identity as the body of Christ, by the Spirit's power. If there is no organized way of using Scripture in worship and education, then there is a tendency for leaders to play to their favorite themes and texts, making their own interests master over the biblical texts. Yet, on the other hand, there is not a single "surefire" method for using Scripture in worship that automatically leads to fidelity to the gospel.

The ministry of Word and sacrament is at the heart of the church's identity because the triune drama of God is "*really present* in the life of the church, and the liturgy helps us to see, taste, imagine, and *live* it."[17] Our lives our not our own, but belong to the living Christ through the Holy Spirit, and in the church's worshipful celebration, the source and identity of our true life is spoken, heard, tasted, and felt. Worship is not constituted by a set of personal preferences resulting in a "traditional" or "contemporary" style. Worship is defined by God and his word, coming to us in the divine drama. In worship, the Spirit

17 Kevin Vanhoozer, *The Drama of Doctrine: A Canonical-Linguistic Approach to Christian Theology* (Louisville: Westminster John Knox, 2005), 410.

enlivens the people of God to participate in Christ, in gratitude to the Father.

CHAPTER 9

The Jesus Way in Divided Times

Kristen Deede Johnson

The divisions we have experienced in the United States in recent years are deep and real. They show no signs of abating. Given the levels of discord we see all around us, many are genuinely and rightly asking whether we in the United States have the resources to sustain our collective political life. Here, I want to ask a more focused question: what resources can we look to as Christians seeking to live the Jesus way here and now, in this contentious time?

Years ago, I was involved in a research project on globalization. When one of our researchers asked a vice president of a major American multinational corporation how his company thought about selling their product in a global market, the vice president answered, "Oh, we're not selling a product. We're selling a way of life."

A stark but honest admission. We are surrounded by forces that, either intentionally or unintentionally, shape our way of life. In the U.S., Christians have been rightly concerned about the impact of forces like consumer capitalism as they shape the desires of Christians and thereby impacts Christians' ways of living in the world. Most recently, we have become deeply aware of the shaping impact of our polarized and divided political reality.

As Christians, we are seeking to live a certain way of life, a way of life to which we believe God has called us. References to this way are woven throughout Scripture, from God's call to Abraham ("For I have chosen him, that he may charge his children and his household after him to keep the way of the Lord by doing righteousness and justice" [Genesis 18:19]) to Proverbs (with its frequent admonitions to seek the way of wisdom, the way of the good, the path of the righteous), Jesus ("I am the way, and the truth, and the life" [John 14:6]), and the earliest believers in Acts (called "followers of the Way"). Eugene Peterson calls this simply "the Jesus Way."

The challenges in our political society are not going to be overcome quickly or easily. What does it mean to live the Jesus Way in this complex, contentious, and divided moment?

Taking the Long View

As we begin to consider this question, I invite us to take the long view. In a very real sense, followers of the Way have been grappling with the relationship between their faith and their political realities since the time of Jesus. "Our citizenship," Paul writes, "is in heaven, and it is from there that we are expecting a Savior, the Lord Jesus Christ" (Philippians 3:20). At the same time, Paul calls us to "be subject to the governing authorities; for there is no authority except from God" (Romans 13:1). Saint Augustine, writing three centuries later, famously drew on these biblical notions to remind Christians that we need to attend to two cities: the heavenly city and the earthly city. The earthly cities of which we're a part might seem more real and more shaping, but for Christians, our primary citizenship is in the heavenly city of which Christ is king. That ought to be the most shaping reality for us, no matter what is going on around us—even the fall of Rome.

It's hard for us today to recognize how significant it was for Augustine and others of his day to live through the fall of the city of Rome, with all of its political and religious significance. The shock experienced, the questions raised, the instability introduced, the explanations offered, the divisions present. While this is by no means an exact parallel to our day, we can take comfort in being surrounded by a great cloud of witnesses, and we ought to find it encouraging that Christians like Augustine lived through political turmoil in their earthly cities and were able to retain their hope in Christ the King.

Historically, it might also be an encouragement to remember that there is no "ideal" configuration between the heavenly city and our earthly cities that we can look to within our past. The earliest Christians lived in what is often termed "the age of the martyrs" because of the suffering they experienced within the political regime of the Roman empire. After Constantine, we see essentially 1500 years of Christian experimentation in relations between what we today call "church" and "state." Christians explored different configurations between bishops, emperors, popes, and other political authorities—all complicated again by the Reformation.

Eventually, we get to the American experiment, the first deliberate attempt to create a political society in which religion had no official role. And yet, because the U.S. was overwhelmingly Protestant at the time of its founding, we were left with enduring questions related to the place of the church in political life. Things like Sunday legislation related to keeping the Sabbath, laws prohibiting atheism, and religious tests for officeholders were all considered acceptable even without an established church. Then the religious awakenings of the nineteenth century led to a prominent evangelical Protestant sensibility within our country.

In very broad brushstrokes, this Protestant sensibility infamously fractured in what we have come to call the modernist-fundamentalist divide, which emerged in the twentieth century. In light of economic and cultural shifts associated with industrialization and urbanization, as well as intellectual movements that challenged traditional Christian doctrine and interpretations of Scripture, two main Protestant responses emerged. Modernists believed that Christian faith should adjust to the new shape, developments, and norms of modern life. Fundamentalists were committed to resisting modernist reinterpretations and to holding to the fundamentals of their faith. For most fundamentalists, this led to a season of withdrawal from public life and mainstream institutions. This meant that although divisions were real, they were a bit hidden for a season.

Fast-forward to the 1940s and 1950s. A convert to Christianity, Carl F. H. Henry, starts to ask questions about this posture of separation and withdrawal. He observes from his study of Christian history that traditional Christians were always socially engaged, but not so in his day. He issues a prophetic call to fundamentalists to come out of their cultural hibernation, noting that "For the first protracted period in its history, evangelical Christianity stands divorced from the great social reform movements."[1] He calls Christians to re-engage on a range

1 Carl F. H. Henry, *The Uneasy Conscience of Modern Fundamentalism* (Grand Rapids, MI: Eerdmans, 2003), 27.

of issues, and to do so with a very different posture from the typical fundamentalist one. He urged Christians, for example, to penetrate and persuade America rather than confront it.

As he joined with others like Billy Graham (who became the gentle and winsome public face of this movement), they launched a new movement that became known as neo-evangelicalism. This included the creation of a number of new institutions and entities to support and promote this cultural re-engagement, from *Christianity Today* to the National Association of Evangelicals, World Relief, Fuller Theological Seminary, and Gordon-Conwell Theological Seminary.

This evangelical re-engagement was not primarily political in nature, nor was it focused on a narrow range of issues. (To provide one example, Henry suggests that evangelical Christians ought to be concerned about "aggressive warfare, racial hatred and intolerance, the liquor traffic, and exploitation of labor and management.")[2]

In the 1970s and 1980s, however, we see the emergence of more overtly political engagement by traditional White Christians. Known as the Religious Right, this movement can in some senses be seen as one way of responding to Henry's prophetic call for re-engagement, while in other ways it harkened back to the fundamentalist posture that Henry was urging Christians of his day to resist. As political scientist David K. Ryden notes, this movement was "defensive in nature, characterized by an 'us against them' mentality' and a 'culture under attack mindset.'"[3] Their political engagement was motivated by a sense of moral and cultural shifts which they rejected. The phrase "Moral Majority" was supposed to capture this: we may have been quiet on the political front, but we are in fact here, we represent a significant portion of the population, and we have moral disagreements with the changes we see all around us. And we are now prepared to fight for what we believe is right.

These Christians were indeed right that significant differences existed within the American population. As political conflicts erupted in the 1980s over unexpected things like funding for the arts and education, alongside abortion and the family, political commentators and journalists were struggling to make sense of the animosity and division they were witnessing. James Davison Hunter turned

2 Henry, *The Uneasy Conscience*, 4.

3 David K. Ryden, "The Good Book as Policy Guide: Characteristics, Critiques, and Contributions of Evangelical Public Policy Participation," in *Is the Good Book Good Enough*, ed. David K. Ryden (Lanham, MD: Lexington Books, 2011), 242.

to a German term to help provide clarity: we were in the midst of a *kulturkampf*, a "culture war." This provided a new lens through which to view our country's conflict.

Rather than being fueled by economic or religious differences, which had been typical ways of understanding cultural conflict, Hunter argued that our conflict was emerging from fundamental differences in systems of moral understanding. What are the sources of our moral authority? How do we determine what is right or wrong, acceptable or unacceptable? "Progressives," as Hunter describes them, view truth as an ever-unfolding reality that should reshape our received traditions and categories. (You can see some resonance here with the modernist perspective that emerged in the 1920s that we ought to shape and change our traditions as modern society changes.) By contrast, those who are "orthodox" have a commitment to an external, definable, and transcendent authority. If we probe deep enough to get to these different notions of truth and authority, and then go back up to the political level, we see that these different systems of moral understanding lead to very different political convictions related to the family, marriage, art, education, and so on.

The divisions that Hunter helped to name in the 1980s have only gotten more widespread in the intervening years. No longer confined to the political realm, we are now all deeply aware of the profound divisions in U.S. society. As John Inazu and Tim Keller put it in their recent book *Uncommon Ground*, we now find ourselves in a political society made up of people with "deep and irresolvable differences over the things that matter most."[4]

This is our reality. As I have endeavored to demonstrate in this brief historical overview, these divisions have been building within our collective life for over a century. This means they are not going away anytime soon.

Considering Our Political Witness

This historical narrative at play within American public life is important to acknowledge as we seek to live the Jesus Way today. Alongside the rise of these divisions within our collective life, we also need to acknowledge two other dynamics that impact our calling as followers of Jesus in this political moment.

4 "Introduction," in *Uncommon Ground: Living Faithfully in a World of Difference*, ed. Timothy Keller and John Inazu, (Nashville: Thomas Nelson, 2020), xv.

First, in recent decades we have seen the increasing politicization of the U.S. In reality, U.S. culture is made up of a number of different institutions, but politics has come to take up more and space in our collective life. Among other things, this means it has become increasingly difficult to imagine our public life, as well as solutions to social and public issues, in non-political terms.

Second, alongside the politicization of U.S. society, we have seen a rise in a particular mode of political engagement shared by all political perspectives. The term "culture wars" speaks to this mode, marked as it is by a sense of embattlement, a call to fight for what is right, and a competition among factions, with the goal being to dominate rather than to persuade. James Davison Hunter has described this at length in his recent book *To Change the World,* noting that our political culture is currently dominated by such Nietzschean sensibilities as the will to power and *ressentiment.* It has become, he writes, "far easier to force one's will on others through legal and political means or to threaten to do so than it is to persuade them or negotiate compromise with them."[5]

This increased politicization combined with a mode of political engagement marked by a will to power are true across the board. In other words, generally speaking we have all become increasingly political and combative in our cultural engagement in the past few decades, regardless of our side or party. This is a widespread mode of engagement that has also shaped White evangelical Christians. That is to say, White evangelical Christians, broadly speaking, have not resisted this mode of engagement. They have not offered a distinctive witness. They have not, to use Paul's words in Romans 12, resisted the pattern of this world when it comes to their political engagement.

Or, as Hunter puts it even more strongly, "With the reduction of the public to the political and the subsequent politicization of so much of human experience, there is an accommodation to the spirit of the age that has made politics the dominant witness of the church to the world."[6]

Hunter is certainly not the only one pointing this out. More recently, evangelical insider Kaitlyn Schiess has reflected on the degree to which White evangelical Christians have been formed by their political engagement and calls on us to pause, take stock, and seek

5 James Davison Hunter, *To Change the World: The Irony, Tragedy, and Possibility of Christianity in the Late Modern World* (New York: Oxford University Press, 2010), 107.

6 Hunter, *To Change the World*, 173.

formation into a different way.[7] Political scientist Amy Black has been reminding us for years that, as she writes, "Politics and government are important, but the most important Christian calling is to love God and follow him."[8] She calls us to understand politics as a way to demonstrate love in action. Black reminds us that 1 Corinthians 13, the famous "love chapter" of the Bible, does not have a political caveat.

Let's pause to read some of those words of Paul on love as we consider our collective, and perhaps even our personal, political witness today:

> Love is patient, love is kind. It does not envy, it does not boast, it is not proud. It does not dishonor others, it is not self-seeking, it is not easily angered, it keeps no record of wrongs. Love does not delight in evil but rejoices with the truth. It always protects, always trusts, always hopes, always perseveres. (1 Corinthians 13:4-7)

These words provide a beautiful picture of love in action, written to a church in conflict. How might they help orient us today, as we seek to live the Jesus way in our own divided settings?

Augustine pointedly suggests that we do not actually understand the Bible if we are not embodying what he calls the "double love of God and neighbor" that is attested to in the pages of the Bible: "So anyone who thinks that he has understood the divine scriptures or any part of them, but cannot by his understanding build up this double love of God and neighbor, has not yet succeeded in understanding them."[9]

We know that love of neighbor is an integral part of our calling as Christians. We have to go about loving our neighbors in ways that embody love as the Bible attests to it, in ways that 1 Corinthians 13 points to. Jesus told us that "you will know them by their fruits" (Matthew 7:16), and Paul draws on the same imagery to articulate the fruit of the Spirit in Galatians 5: love, joy, peace, patience, kindness, goodness, faithfulness, gentleness, and self-control.

Let's remember, though, that embodying the fruit of the Spirit is not something we can do on our own. As Christians, that is true all the

7 Kaitlyn Schiess, *The Liturgy of Politics: Spiritual Formation for the Sake of Our Neighbor* (Downers Grove, IL: InterVarsity Press, 2020).

8 Amy E. Black, *Honoring God in Red or Blue: Approaching Politics with Humility, Grace, and Reason* (Chicago: Moody Publishers, 2012), 19.

9 Augustine, *On Christian Teaching*, trans. R. P. H. Green (Oxford: Oxford University Press, 2008), I.36.40.

time, but we need to recognize that this is even more so with all of the cultural and political forces pushing us towards polarization. These forces are like a current that will inevitably, perhaps at times ever so subtly, carry us along towards divisiveness unless we, with God's help, seek a different way. And, thanks be to God, he has given us the Spirit. By the Spirit's power and grace, we can bear the fruit of the Spirit and live the Jesus Way, even in our political engagement.

To help us live the Jesus way in this polarized time, with God's help, I want to offer a few suggestions.

Learn Each Other's Stories (In All Their Complexity)

One way we can embody the Jesus Way is by taking time to learn each other's stories and to complexify the stories we are both receiving and telling.

Lecrae reminds us in a recent essay that as humans we create narratives that provide a way of making sense of the world and of events that take place in this world. As we create and find these stories, we tend to be drawn towards narratives that fit with the beliefs, convictions, and frameworks that we already have. As Lecrae puts it, "people gravitate toward a story that aligns with their current way of seeing the world. It's our default setting."[10] Social psychologist Jonathan Haidt has drawn attention to this phenomenon through his long-term research on how people develop and justify their beliefs, noting that intuition tends to come first and rational thought, which helps to justify those intuitions, comes second.[11] Because of these tendencies, it's hard for us to have our own minds changed, as well as to change other people's mind. It takes intentional commitment to be open to questioning and complexifying the stories we are telling.

Right now, many of the cultural and political stories we are receiving and telling are overly simplistic. As Lecrae points out, these stories have very clear heroes and very obvious villains, but if you have a different perspective, those heroes and villains flip. He explores interpretations of events in Ferguson, Missouri, in light of this hero-villain framework and tellingly points out just how different the renditions of that story become.

As Christians, we ought to be the most equipped to complexify these stories. We know that all have sinned and fall short of the glory

10 Lecrae, "The Storyteller," in *Uncommon Ground*, 104.

11 Jonathan Haidt, *The Righteous Mind: Why Good People Are Divided by Politics and Religion* (New York: Vintage Books, 2013).

of God, so this should make it impossible to tell a story in which a particular person or political figure (or a particular demographic, series of events, or political party) is either a clear villain or a straightforward hero. As Aleksandr Solzhenitsyn famously wrote, "The line separating good and evil passes not through states, nor between classes, nor between political parties either, but right through every human heart, and through all human hearts."[12]

For Christians, we understand that only Jesus Christ is the true hero. This, combined with the larger story of Scripture, ought to equip us to do the hard work of complexifying the simplistic stories that often mark this cultural moment. We are called to do the wrestling that enables us to see both the sinful realities and the signs of redemption and grace that come with acknowledging Jesus Christ as Lord, Savior, and King, the one who has reconciled all things (Colossians 1) and who continues the work of reconciliation as he makes all things news (Revelation 21).

To help us do this wrestling, we will need to take time. This involves slowing down to learn more about the stories behind the "characters" that are presented to us as either wholly right or wholly wrong within our current cultural scripts. It includes, as Lecrae notes, having the humility to listen and to learn from others and about others, rather than assuming we know.[13] It will also involve taking the time to widen our sources. As we often hear now, the sources we each regularly consult tend to tell and reinforce certain stories and interpretations. While it's certainly okay to have sources you trust and regularly consult, intentionally engaging with a wide range of sources can help with this work of complexifying the stories we are both receiving and telling. This might include moving beyond typical news sources to read thoughtful novels and watch movies and documentaries that can help us enter into different people's stories and backgrounds.

When We Disagree, Go Deeper

As we seek to live the Jesus Way in this time of deep difference, we ought to expect disagreement to arise in our interactions with others. When we encounter these disagreements, we need to go even deeper.

Just as we want to recognize that there are no simplistic stories with straightforward heroes and villains, we also must acknowledge

12 Aleksandr Solzhenitsyn, *The Gulag Archipelago*, vol. 2 (New York: Harper and Row, 1975), 615–16.

13 Lecrae, "The Storyteller," 103.

that political and cultural issues are themselves complex. Christians have been disagreeing about important issues since before they were called Christians. The New Testament is full of stories of the earliest followers of the Way wrestling and disagreeing. The same will be true of us today. Even if we hone in on just the last few decades in the U.S. context, we will come to see that the expectation that all Christians would belong to one political party or coalesce clearly around one political issue or set of issues is a fairly recent one. (And, of course, the political parties themselves, their positions, and who tends to support them, regionally and otherwise, have also shifted over time.)

Here we come back to the question of our posture: if we expect disagreement because these issues are complex, what is the appropriate posture for us to have in the midst of these disagreements? How can we continue to embody the way of Jesus even when we encounter disagreements? One answer lies in going deeper. Recognizing that we live in a time of deep difference, can we be intentional about going deep ourselves to try to understand what's beneath the disagreements we are encountering?

The Colossian Forum is animated by the conviction that because in Christ all things hold together, we don't have to be afraid our differences. The Colossian Forum provides resources to congregations and other Christian communities with the hope that God can turn divisions into opportunities for discipleship. Through one of their resources, the Colossian Way, small groups of Christians are invited to wrestle with divisive issues together, including politics. If you participate in the Colossian Way, you are encouraged to ask two questions every time you encounter anger in someone with whom you disagree: *What is the fear beneath the anger?* and *What is the love beneath the fear?*

These are questions we all need to be asking as we seek to live the Jesus Way. When we encounter disagreement with and anger in another, can we pause to drill down further? Can we try to uncover what fear might be behind and beneath the anger? Going deeper still, what is positive that that person or movement loves and is trying to preserve? What do they think is at stake? What are they afraid of losing? What do they fear is changing?

I'd encourage us to go deep in our own self-reflection as well. When we feel the anger swelling in us, can we ask ourselves what is beneath that anger? What is the fear fueling that anger? What is the love driving that fear?

And we ought to add into this mix that fear and anger are often used as political motivators in this cultural moment. Groups and figures on both sides regularly tap into fears and angers to mobilize people for engagement. When we witness this happening, can we, as Christians, ask God to help us place our fears into the larger context of the hope we have in Christ?

Keep Politics in Its Place

With this reminder of our hope being firmly rooted in Christ, we also need to remember to keep politics in its proper place.

Our hope does not lie in a particular president or political party. Our hope does not depend upon any certain outcome in an election. Our hope lies in Jesus Christ, and only in Christ can this hope be firm and secure as an anchor for the soul (Hebrews 6).

Idolatry has always come easy to us, hence the need for the first commandment. Today our idols can be more subtle than in other times and places, but any time we place our hope and trust in something other than God, we run the risk of turning that thing into a god. Politics has an important place within our collective life, but it needs to stay in its place. As I noted above, we have seen the politicization of American society. More and more our understanding of societal life together takes place through politics. Part of our Christian witness today can lie in offering a different way.

Politics is not the only or even the most important institution in our society. Nor, for Christians, ought it to be the main venue for our public engagement. As Hunter writes, "At best, the state's role addressing in human problems is partial and limited. It is not nearly as influential as the expectations most people have of it."[14] Hunter notes that Christians have invested considerable energy, time, and money into the political arena in the last few decades, thinking that was the way to change the world. Tragically, that is not the main way to enact cultural change. Nor is Hunter convinced that cultural change ought to be our animating goal as Christians.

If we seek wisdom from Augustine as we think about our political engagement, we want to take our pilgrimage in this earthly city seriously. Augustine urged the Christians of his day to do this by seeking the welfare of the cities in which they resided, drawing on the words of Jeremiah, and in doing so, he said, they would find a shared

14 Hunter, *To Change the World*, 173.

earthly peace. Even with this encouragement, he never wanted them to conflate the earthly city and its earthly peace with the city of God and its heavenly peace rooted in the Prince of Peace. He did not want politics to be the source of hope for redemption and salvation of this world's problems, but pointed the Christians of his day to Christ for that hope.

Be Like Trees

In my years of reflecting on what the Jesus Way looks like in complex cultural times, I have increasingly turned to our calling within Scripture to be like trees (Psalm 1). Deeply rooted in the living waters of Christ (John 4), knit together as fellow citizens of God's kingdom and members of God's household (Ephesians 2), what if our witness to the world was that of trees which offer life-giving oxygen to the world, along with beauty, shade, fruit, protection, and places to play?

Trees offer these life-giving gifts to all around them, not only to their own kind. They are rooted in one location and make that particular place better by their very presence. And with deep roots, trees can develop wide branches that enable them to find places of overlap with other branches, even branches that come from different kinds of trees with their own deep roots.

This sounds like the Jesus Way—to be people who offer life to the world, rooted in Christ rather than fear or despair, attentive to our local places, discerning how we might offer life-giving oxygen, fruit, shade, and sustenance to the people and institutions around us, generously finding places of overlap rather than demarcating lines of division. By their fruit you shall know them. May our leaves contribute to the healing of the nations (Revelation 22). May we, by God's grace bear the fruit of the Spirit in the world.

A Reflection on One Tree: Tim Brown

As I consider this biblical calling to be like trees, I find myself reflecting on one person who has been like a tree throughout his years of ministry and institutional service: Timothy L. Brown. Tim is deeply rooted in Christ, which frees him to interact with love and generosity with Christians who hold very different convictions than his own. Tim is attentive to the local places to which God calls him: he was committed to local church ministry for decades before investing deeply in the ecosystem of Western Theological Seminary through his presence and intentional service. Tim breathed life-giving oxygen into the places he was called to serve and into the people he befriended and served in those places. Each church and institution emerged stronger, healthier, and more full of the life of Christ because of his leadership, preaching, and pastoral presence.

The divisions that we've been reflecting on in this essay certainly impacted the churches and institutions that Tim was given to shepherd. Yet Tim navigated these divisions with 1 Corinthians 13 love and Galatians 5 fruit of the Spirit. In his engagement with others, Tim was formed not by the larger cultural climate of conflict and anger, but by the witness of Scripture. He embodied the Jesus Way.

The work of the Holy Spirit in forming and sanctifying us is mysterious. That being said, I would venture to suggest that Tim's years of immersion in the holy Scriptures and in the worshiping life of local churches were means of grace used by the Spirit to shape Tim to be like a tree.

For decades, Tim has interiorized the words of Scripture, meditated on them, allowed them to bear fruit in his own life, and offered wisdom, truth, and beauty from them to the wider church through his significant preaching ministry. Through his regular involvement in church and seminary worship and his commitment to the weekly practice of the Lord's Supper, the Spirit shaped his imagination to be attentive to the deeper realities of the kingdom of God—the City of God, to use Augustine's language—even as he was shaped to engage with love, patience, and generosity in the daily realities of life in this world.

As God worked through the practices of Scripture interiorization, worship in the local church, and the Lord's Supper to help Tim embody the Jesus Way, God by his grace can do so for the rest of us, to help us to live the Jesus Way, to be like trees, in this complex and polarized moment.

A Closing Prayer

Lord, as we await the day of the City of God, give us wisdom to know how to live the Jesus Way in this divided time. Thank you for the witness of those like Tim Brown, who have embodied the Jesus Way and from whom we can learn as we try to live differently in this world, in this cultural moment. Give us the strength and patience to be like trees, with deep roots in you, sustained by the living waters of your Son, and bearing the fruit of your Spirit that can only come by the grace and power of your Spirit at work in us. Help us—help all of your people—to be known by the life we offer this world. Help us to be deeply attentive to the places that need your shalom and to be discerning about how you might use us to participate in your ongoing work of redemption, right where we are. Help us, Lord, to be like trees.

CHAPTER 10

"Pastor, Preacher, Parent: But the greatest of these is...": An essay for pastors and preachers who are also parents on the occasion of my dad's retirement

Jon Brown

Eugene Peterson, early in his book *Like Dew Your Youth,* offers these provocative words: "There are no techniques to master that will make a good parent. There is no book to read that will give the right answers."[1] With Peterson's cautionary words in my mind, far be it from me in the next 5000 words, with four children under the age of 15 living in my home, and all the questions, concerns, anxieties, hopes, and joys that Kristyn (my beloved wife) and I experience on a daily basis, to pretend to offer some sort of "here's-how-to-do-it" parenting program. I am reluctant to offer any sort of definitive word on how to parent in general, let alone parent in such a way that our kids grow up to love Jesus, the church, and the world that God loves. I would, however, like to burrow with you, for just a little while, down into the great words of the apostle Paul, and see if we can come back up to the light of day with some clues for raising our kids decently (and "in good order" if you're of the Reformed tradition).

1 Eugene Peterson, *Like Dew Your Youth: Growing Up with Your Teenager* (Grand Rapids, MI: Eerdmans, 1976), 10.

Paul writes,

> "Love is patient; love is kind; love is not envious or boastful or arrogant or rude. It does not insist on its own way; it is not irritable or resentful; it does not rejoice in wrongdoing, but rejoices in the truth. It bears all things, believes all things, hopes all things, endures all things. Love never ends." (1 Corinthians 13:4-8a)

I'd like to borrow from that crescendo on love and offer a modest invitation to parents who are also pastors and preachers: "Love bears all things, believes all things, hopes all things, endures all things. Love never ends."

I grew up a pastor's kid. I remember pretty clearly the knowing look of sarcasm in the eyes of those who were learning for the first time of my plight as pastor's kid, the look that assumed some sort of hellish behavior on my part. I was a pastor's kid, after all, and we're notoriously disruptive, maybe second only to missionary kids. We're so notorious we go simply by the letters *PK*. I can remember in my spirit the desire to prove them right. If it wasn't the look of an assumption that I would be bad, then it was the look assuming I'd be especially good. I "knew better," for Pete's sake. I was being raised right. If I couldn't be a good Christian kid, how in the world was my buddy, especially the one who went to a public school, supposed to get by? I can still remember in my heart the desire to prove popular opinion wrong. Sometimes—and this was worse for me—the struggle was not being noticed at all. Upon hearing I was a pastor's kid, all I'd hear about was my dad. "We love your dad." "Your dad is an amazing preacher; do you know that?" "What's it like to have your dad as your parent?" "You're so lucky to have your dad." Those are the whispers that kept me quiet. It's hard to say anything when no one knows you're there.

Wonderfully, none of those responses were any real reflection on my dad. Peterson adds in the same book, "A parent's main job is not to be a parent, but to be a person."[2] That was my dad. He was a person for me. He'd come home from work, and frankly I didn't care what work he was doing; I was just glad he was home. He'd come home from work, roll up his sleeves, and challenge me to a best- of-ten free-throw contest. He was a person. After dinner ("please, Dad, make it a short prayer") and before an evening meeting I'd challenge him to a best-of-three ping-pong match, which usually ended in a wrestling match too.

2 Peterson, *Like Dew Your Youth*, 10.

He was a person. On the way to school in the morning (this was before coffee shops) he'd give me 52 cents to run into Jackie's restaurant and get him a cup of coffee, half decaf, half regular (I now understand why the half-decaf). He was a person. That was the best part of my dad for me. His call as pastor and his gifts as preacher are something to behold and be celebrated, and I don't mean to diminish either in any way. But I just wanted a dad. I just needed a person.

Now I'm a pastor and a preacher and a parent. I feel every tug of pastoral ministry to be more and to do better, to be available for every pastoral call, hospital visit, and religious occasion. People laugh when they hear how Stanley Hauerwas describes the pastor as a "quivering mass of availability," but I shudder.[3] I know it so well. I feel every pressure to give my best as a preacher, because the gospel of Christ deserves my best efforts. I love the words of encouragement, the stories of growth, and the reflections of what God's Spirit does in a person's life through the preaching of the Word. I believe both pastor and preacher are instrumentally significant in the work God is accomplishing in the world. (I believe that same thing about nearly every profession.) I also know deep in my bones that my kids don't really care. They care, I guess—they're not opposed to the pastor or preacher, but they want a person. My kids are aware of the privilege they experience. They know an occasional trip to Florida in January so Dad can preach is not normal. They realize the special invitation to the lake house, or for the boat ride, or to the museum are curiously connected to Dad's role as pastor and preacher, and they love it, but they still just want a person.

This became horrifyingly clear to me a few weeks ago. Our four-year-old daughter Ava wanted me to play with her. Maybe it was dolls, or tag, or hide-and-seek. But I had a meeting. I had to get going. And my four-year-old daughter who can't yet recite the alphabet or count to ten said, without hesitation, "Dad, you're too busy." Ava wasn't looking for a pastor or a preacher. In that moment she was looking for a person, a dad, who had time for tag and dolls and the most banal game of hide-and-seek known to humankind, where hiding is optional and seeking isn't necessary. My dad had meetings too. Surely he did. He had responsibilities to balance. Somebody had to answer the phone when Bob (the guy who called us collect from prison what seemed like every night during dinner) wanted to talk to my dad. Somebody had to do the weddings and the funerals and lead the consistory meeting. I

3 Qtd. in William Willimon, *Pastor: The Theology and Practice of Ordained Ministry* (Nashville: Abingdon Press, 2002), 60.

realize my dad did all those things, but what I remember is that he was a person first. He was pastor, your beloved preacher. But he was always a person for me. That is something I always wanted to honor. For example, when Kristyn and I got married, I didn't ask him to officiate our wedding. Even though he was actually my pastor and he's the best preacher I can think of, it was more fitting for him to sit next to my mom during the wedding. I wanted him to be my dad who was not just a role model or an ecclesial function, but a person who was loved.

I wonder if 1 Corinthians 13:4-8 gives us a vision of how to parent as a person—not a pastor or preacher, but a person. "[Love] bears all things, believes all things, hopes all things, endures all things. Love never ends." Paul is not writing specifically to parents (nor is he writing just to brides and grooms); he's writing to anyone and everyone who counts themselves a part of the church, who has received the stunning gift of following Christ in life, faith, and mission. If he's talking to all of us who love Jesus, then it must mean that he's also talking to each of us who have been given the unspeakably wonderful, and mostly overwhelming, gift of raising children as parents.

Love Bears All Things: Permission

Your beloved child, sooner or later, is going to make a mistake. It probably won't even be a mistake; it will be an outright grievance, a transgression, a sin. She's going to mess it up. She's going to either do or say something that runs contrary to your heart for her as a person and as a Christian. And sometimes it won't just be a private opportunity to teach a lesson but will have an impact on the church. Your reputation as a church leader will feel like it's on the line. Your reputation as a Christian parent will feel like it's at stake. Her actions may result in church tension or even people leaving your church. Peterson asks,

> Does good parenting guarantee good children? A lot of parents assume that it does: that if we do a responsible and intelligent job as mothers and fathers, if we provide a Christian home and are faithful in our prayers, if we raise our children "in the nurture and admonition of the Lord," our children are going to turn out well. But there are precious few facts to support the assumption.... [Parents] are apt to interpret every deviation from their teaching as evidence of parental failure.[4]

[4] Peterson, *Like Dew Your Youth,* 100–01.

"Love bears all things." The word I want to give to this orientation is *permission*. Our tendency is to make our kids a reflection of ourselves. If they're good, I'm good. If they're well behaved, I'm a good parent. If people speak well of them, they think well of me. That is a pressure a child is not meant to carry. They need permission to try, risk, go, challenge, speak, wonder. They need permission to ask and to be curious and to fail. If "love bears all things," we can give our kids permission to learn and grow and become outside the confines of our expectations and the pressure of meeting our reputation's needs.

When I was in high school, there was an adult Sunday school class on parenting. Someone must have thought it was a good idea to invite some high schoolers to share their experiences, and someone must have thought it was a good idea for me to be one of the high schoolers to share his experience. I have no idea what my panel of friends and I said to our parents on that day, and I highly doubt anyone else does either, but I do remember that one person (it might have been me), when asked for one last thought, said, "You have to give us space to make some mistakes." Adolescent Jon wasn't looking to run roughshod over our family's values or disregard our convictions; he simply wanted permission to become, to grow, and even to fail as a way to maturity. I like the way Peterson puts it: "'Grace' does not preclude pain and bewilderment–biblically, it usually includes it. But God-ordained means of grace, regardless of appearances, and any feelings we might have toward them at the time, get us to the end that God intends for us, in this case, the 'measure of the stature of the fulness of Christ.'"[5] "Love bears all things."

Love Believes All Things: Passion

I don't understand exactly what the apostle Paul means by "Love believes all things." Surely the Christian faith doesn't believe *all things*. It actually makes some fairly exclusive claims, like "Jesus Christ is Lord." I do wonder, though, if what Paul has in mind is not a doctrinal belief in matters of ultimate meaning, but rather a charitable belief in the image of God-ness in the other (in this case our kids) and in the Spirit's redeeming work in their lives. Love believes that, though your son doesn't seem to be "acting himself these days," or is doing things that aren't in line with "the way that he should go," he is a beloved child of God, and the Spirit of Christ is active in the world, redeeming and reclaiming your son to Christ.

5 Peterson, *Like Dew Your Youth*, 5.

Historically, there has been a pretty significant battle in child psychology between the "Focus on the Family" conviction of discipline as the way to raise up a child and Dr. Benjamin Spock's more lenient ways of parenting flexibility and affection. I'm not entering that battle here. I'm inviting each of us as parent-persons to believe in the work of God in our children's lives. This is what the liturgy would have us say when we baptize the youngest among us: "It was for you that Christ came into the world, it was for you that he died. It was for you that he rose again, yes for you, little one, even though you may know nothing of it yet. We love because God first loved us."[6]

The word I want to give to this orientation of love is *passion*. Passion not as an excited energy, but as a willingness to see more than the circumstances are presenting. My dad is known for his love of and ability to tell stories. Who among us, if you've heard it, doesn't love the Tim VanderVeen story: "Life isn't like a VCR; you can't fast-forward the bad parts"? Or the Art Smallegan story: "You forgot to read." Or the story of the woman in the hospital who saw Jesus in her hospital room: "He had dark skin and deep brown eyes. He was wearing a stethoscope and a white coat." We love his stories, but what is better than the story is the passion to see more than what's most obviously there. Can you see the redemptive work of Christ in your child's life? Will you see the Spirit drawing your son to Jesus? Do you notice the gospel claim on your daughter, even in the most trying circumstance: "I have called you by name, you are mine" (Isaiah 43:1)? "Love believes all things."

Love Hopes All Things: Apology

We hope that if we put the right guidelines in place, find the right people to surround them, and get them into the right schools, then our kids will turn out right. That's not hope; that's control. I'm not dismissing those aspects as important, but hope is something else. *Hope* is the confident expectation that Jesus is who he says he is and will accomplish what he says he'll do. This forces us as parents to be honest. We don't have to hide from our kids the insecurities we carry, the weaknesses we know, and the failures and shortcomings we have. We don't have to have it all together and get it all right to ensure that our kids grow up happy, healthy, and wise. To borrow again from Peterson, reflecting on parenting adolescents,

6 *Combined Order for Baptism, Profession of Faith and Reaffirmation of Faith,* Reformed Church in America, accessed December 29, 2020, https://www.rca.org/liturgy/combined-order-for-baptism-profession-of-faith-and-reaffirmation-of-faith/.

> Parents of adolescents, it seems to me, are not at their best when they do the right things or say the right things, but when, in faith, they plunge into the process of growth....
>
> [Parents] don't have to be experts in psychology or to have read the latest book on adolescent emotions, and they don't have to live perfect lives, but they must take seriously what they are doing, which is growing up in Christ. They must do it openly before adolescents so that the adolescents can observe, imitate, and make mistakes in the context of care and faith.[7]

We hope in a God who reconciles all things to himself and is making all things new, so a parent is invited to live the open life of sin and grace before their child.

The word I want to give to this orientation of love is *apology*. Our kids see us at our most vulnerable. They hear us argue with our spouse. They notice us staying up too late. They see not the pastor nor the preacher but the *person* in all of his or her stunning realness. There's no pulling the wool over their eyes. And if we try, we tend also to invite them to pull the wool over other's eyes. We don't want them to see our shortcomings or to be honest about our sins, and we don't want anyone else to see our sin either. So we dress up for church and we go to great lengths to make sure they're there on time and that they sit quietly. Then they are tempted to develop a duplicitous life: to do one thing at home when no one is looking and another thing at church when everyone is. Sooner or later, they'll break free from the shackles of that inauthenticity. Isn't this what the apostle John wrote so clearly? "If we say that we have no sin, we deceive ourselves, and the truth is not in us. If we confess our sins, he who is faithful and just will forgive us our sins and cleanse us from all unrighteousness" (1 John 1:8-9). If it's generally true for all Christians, it seems also particularly important for Christian parents trying to raise their children. This is uniquely challenging for any of us, especially parents, who are trying to follow Jesus in the world.

If we were more willing to live openly before our kids our up-and-down lives with Christ and say to our kids, "I'm sorry," I wonder if they'd be less constrained by the chains of duplicity. I wonder if they'd get the sense that "love hopes all things." Love doesn't have to hide behind the thin veneer of other people's perception of you. Love invites us to be honest with ourselves and each other because it hopes

7 Peterson, *Like Dew Your Youth*, 8-9.

in the redeeming work of God in our lives. As a kid, I regularly found it comical how misunderstood my dad was. Or at least how little of him other people knew. They saw the orator who could turn a phrase; I saw the dad who, though he wouldn't let me stay up to watch the 1985 Michigan–BYU bowl game, came into my room at every score until the game was over. They saw the robed vicar with the three stripes on his sleeves indicating something important; I saw the guy who repeated the colorful phrases of his childhood that he learned from his block-laying, punch-throwing dad (my Grandpa Brown was a boxer; they called him the "Iron Duke"). They saw the consequences of his gifts in meetings, hospital rooms and the sanctuary; I saw the guy who couldn't wait to get home from church on Sunday night to pour a Diet Coke, pick up some Little Caesars, and watch a "slam-bang thriller" movie where us kids would have to close their eyes a few times. The best part was, not only did I get to watch the movie, but I didn't feel like I had to pretend that we didn't watch it to save some strange face in a world of expectations. It was the gift of honesty born in a context where apology was normal. Love hopes all things.

Love Endures All Things: Empathy

My dad didn't cry a lot, but he cried when Grandma Brown died suddenly of a brain aneurism. He cried when Grandpa Brown died of an angry cancer that took the Iron Duke down without a punch. He cried with my neighbor's family when their son was killed in a plane crash. And he invited us into the pain with him. We knew it hurt. The pressures of his role as pastor and responsibilities of his work as preacher weren't hidden from us. And because they were shared with us, they lost the power to keep him from us. We didn't often go to the hospitals with him. (Though I do remember one time going to visit someone in the hospital with him and getting my arm stuck in the stairwell handrail. All you have to do is twist your arm so your elbow lays flat against the wall and pull up). It wasn't like we knew every detail or even every situation of pastoral challenge. There wasn't some weird conflation between his work and our family's life, but we were given the appropriate glimpse into what's really real. I am, I admit, crossing a parenting line that previous generations might not have crossed. In his book *The Duties of Parents*, a part of the Classics of Reformed Spirituality series, Jacobus Koelman instructs parents this way: "Do not be overly familiar and informal with your children, and do not let them be brash toward you.... Excessive familiarity leads to contempt and invites disobedience. Therefore, maintain a certain distance between you and them, and let them honor that distance."[8]

As pastors (though it's probably true of others too), we run into the risk of forming our children in the way of a plastic Christianity, a clichéd faith marked not by endurance but by platitudes, a faith where the cross is only an ignored and unfortunate short stop on the way to resurrection. The unintended consequence is that pain loses its necessary place in the story of faith, and only gain gets to be publicly acknowledged. The cry of agony from the cross, "My God, my God, why?" has no place in our hearts. We end up launching our children into the world with all kinds of answers but not enough questions to withstand the wiles of the unrelenting disappointments life will provide. I don't mean to be overly pessimistic—on the contrary, sharing with our children the pain we know and other people experience is a tremendous gift. We provide them the opportunity then to experience the Christ whose "power is made perfect in weakness" (1 Corinthians 12:9). We open their ears to hear the God who says, "I've heard your cry, I know your pain, I've seen your suffering, and I've come down to deliver you" (Exodus 3:7-8, paraphrased). Their girlfriend is going to break up with them. Their friend is going to get sick. They will get cut from the team, or even if they don't, their athletic career will eventually come to an end. They will be outsmarted by a brighter student, out-recognized by a better artist, or just outed by someone they thought was their best friend. The church will disappoint our kids too. People in even the loveliest congregations disappoint with shocking regularity. In a strange way, opening our beloved children to pain is a gift, because "love endures all things."

The word I want to give to this orientation of love is *empathy* (please notice how hard I'm working to use words that include the letter P). Experiences of pain, when we're honest about them, and as we face them ourselves and in turn appropriately share them with our children, open us and our children to others in unique and beautiful lives. The great Reformed doctrine of total depravity is the guarantee that people are going to hurt. Even as people share with you their best selves, you can be sure there is pain, sadness, and hurt just below the surface. But naming it and sharing it cultivates empathy, and so the pain, in that way, can be given back to the world as a gift. We open up the possibility of forming our kids in the way of empathy so that

8 Jacobus Koelman, *The Duties of Parents* (Grand Rapids, MI: Baker Academic, 2003), 63.

they might then be willing to see more than the pain, the loss, or the sadness. Instead, they can see Christ in pain, experience Jesus in the loss, come face-to-face with the crucified one in the sadness. "Love endures all things."

Love Never Ends: Presence

I could probably do some theological gymnastics to make sense of those words, "Love never ends." "God is love." God is eternal. So love never ends. But I wonder if the apostle Paul had in mind less a statement about the nature of God than a commitment of our lives. A commitment that we won't quit on each other. That we won't give up on our kids. That we'll keep showing up even when they don't really want us around. That we'll be their biggest fans even when they don't think anyone likes them. That we'll say the hard word even when they think we're too strict. That we'll be relentlessly present to, with, and for them. It's possible that it is more important to the faith formation of your son or daughter for you to get it wrong every once in a while, in an effort to assure them that you are *for* them. "Love never ends."

There are a few signature statements my dad loves to use while preaching: "Listen to this from the book that we love." "God in the flesh but God all the same." And maybe most iconic: "Come with me..." My dad loves to start a story with that phrase: "Come with me to the fourth floor of Butterworth hospital." "Come with me to the south side of Chicago on a rainy Saturday morning." "Come with me to Los Angeles International Airport, Terminal 5." It is his way of involving you in the story he is about to tell. What I love about that line is that he never said it to me, but so regularly *did* it for me. When Christ Memorial Church, the congregation he pastored for twelve years, was one of the fasting-growing congregations in America, he would come with me to Grand Haven Middle School to watch me and my teammates play the Buccaneers in basketball. I would play; he would yell at the referees. When another Sunday evening service had finally finished, he would dart home and come with me to Winding Creek Golf Course or Clearbrook Country Club to beat the sunset with nine holes of golf. When I was in college and imagining what I was going to do with my life, he came with me on a forty-five-hour pick-up truck trip straight to Whidbey Island, Washington, for a cup of coffee. "Love never ends."

The word I want to give to this orientation of love is *presence*. Amid all the competing claims on the pastor's life and the demands of the ministry of preaching, your kid wants to know that you're going to be there. And not just sitting in the stands cheering them on, but showing up for them when the necessary question needs to be asked or the important corrective needs to be offered. In encouragement or challenge, what's consistent is presence. Dietrich Bonhoeffer, in his book *Life Together*, puts it differently, but I think it applies:

> The first service that one owes to others in the fellowship consists in listening to them. Just as love of God begins with listening to His Word, so the beginning of love for the brethren is learning to listen to them. It is God's love for us that He not only gives us His Word but also lends us His ear.
>
> So, it is His work that we do for our brother when we learn to listen to him. Christians, especially ministers, so often think they must always contribute something when they are in the company of others, that this is the one service they have to render. They forget that listening can be a greater service than speaking. Many people are looking for an ear that will listen. They do not find it among Christians, because these Christians are talking where they should be listening.[9]

If that's true for ministers in general, how much truer must it be for pastors and preachers who are also parents engaging with their children. As pastors, we have this insatiable need to say something. As preachers, we get paid to say something. I wonder if our kids are more interested in our presence as listeners. Not that we don't speak or share or say anything at all, but as kids grow up, maybe our words could become less and the time we allow for listening could grow longer. "Love never ends."

There are other stories I could tell. Like the time I drove the car into a telephone pole while my dad was in Chicago with my mom. I called him with great fear and trembling to tell him the news. He responded so calmly over the phone. But when he got home the next day, man, did he let me have it. There are more stories: this wasn't meant to be some sort of act of denying the reality of our lives full of successes and failures. My hope in all of this was to awaken the person in those of us who working the angles of pastoral ministry and staying up with the unrelenting rhythm of weekly preaching, who are also given the unspeakable, even if sometimes overwhelming, gift of raising younger ones. As important as our role as pastor may

9 Dietrich Bonhoeffer, *Life Together* (New York: Harper and Row, 1954), 97–98.

be to our congregation and community, and as necessary as the act of preaching surely is for the life of the church, our kids just want a person. To borrow again from Peterson, "A parent's main job is not to be a parent, but to be a person."[10] And if I can add, a person who loves like this: "Love is patient; love is kind; love is not envious or boastful or arrogant or rude. It does not insist on its own way; it is not irritable or resentful; it does not rejoice in wrongdoing, but rejoices in the truth. It bears all things, believes all things, hopes all things, endures all things. Love never ends" (1 Corinthians 13:4-8a). I'd like to borrow from that crescendo on love and offer a modest invitation to parents who are also pastors and preachers: "Love bears all things, believes all things, hopes all things, endures all things. Love never ends."

In the name of the Father and the Son and the Holy Spirit, amen.

[10] Eugene Peterson, *Like Dew Your Youth* (Grand Rapids, MI: Eerdmans), 10.

Publications in the Historical Series of the Reformed Church in America

The following Historical Series publications may be ordered easily through the Faith Alive web site at www.faithaliveresources.org

The home page has a search the site box. Either enter the specific title or author, or enter "Historical Series" to search for all volumes available. Titles will appear with the option of adding to cart. Books may also be ordered through your local bookstore.

You may also see the full list of titles on the RCA website at:

www.rca.org/series

1. *Ecumenism in the Reformed Church in America*, by Herman Harmelink III (1968)
2. *The Americanization of a Congregation*, by Elton J. Bruins (1970)
3. *Pioneers in the Arab World*, by Dorothy F. Van Ess (1974)
4. *Piety and Patriotism*, edited by James W. Van Hoeven (1976)
5. *The Dutch Reformed Church in the American Colonies*, by Gerald F. De Jong (1978)
6. *Historical Directory of the Reformed Church in America, 1628-1978*, by Peter N. VandenBerge (1978)
7. *Digest and Index of the Minutes of General Synod, 1958-1977*, by Mildred W. Schuppert (1979)
8. *Digest and Index of the Minutes of General Synod, 1906-1957*, by Mildred W. Schuppert (1982)
9. *From Strength to Strength*, by Gerald F. De Jong (1982)
10. *"B. D."*, by D. Ivan Dykstra (1982)
11. *Sharifa*, by Cornelia Dalenburg (1983)
12. *Vision From the Hill*, edited by John W. Beardslee III (1984)
13. *Two Centuries Plus*, by Howard G. Hageman (1984)
14. *Structures for Mission*, by Marvin D. Hoff (1985)

15. *The Church Speaks*, edited by James I. Cook (1985)
16. *Word and World*, edited by James W. Van Hoeven (1986)
17. *Sources of Secession: The Netherlands Hervormde Kerk on the Eve of the Dutch Immigration to the Midwest*, by Gerrit J. tenZythoff (1987)
18. *Vision for a Christian College*, by Gordon J. Van Wylen (1988)
19. *Servant Gladly*, edited by Jack D. Klunder and Russell L. Gasero (1989)
20. *Grace in the Gulf*, by Jeanette Boersma (1991)
21. *Ecumenical Testimony*, by Arie R. Brouwer (1991)
22. *The Reformed Church in China, 1842-1951*, by Gerald F. De Jong (1992)
23. *Historical Directory of the Reformed Church in America, 1628-1992*, by Russell L. Gasero (1992)
24. *Meeting Each Other in Doctrine, Liturgy, and Government*, by Daniel J. Meeter (1993)
25. *Gathered at Albany*, by Allan J. Janssen (1995)
26. *The Americanization of a Congregation*, 2nd ed., by Elton J. Bruins (1995)
27. *In Remembrance and Hope: The Ministry and Vision of Howard G. Hageman*, by Gregg A. Mast (1998)
28. *Deacons' Accounts, 1652-1674, First Dutch Reformed Church of Beverwyck/Albany*, trans. & edited by Janny Venema (1998)
29. *The Call of Africa*, by Morrill F. Swart (1998)
30. *The Arabian Mission's Story: In Search of Abraham's Other Son*, by Lewis R. Scudder III (1998)
31. *Patterns and Portraits: Women in the History of the Reformed Church in America*, edited by Renée S. House and John W. Coakley (1999)
32. *Family Quarrels in the Dutch Reformed Churches in the Nineteenth Century*, by Elton J. Bruins & Robert P. Swierenga (1999)
33. *Constitutional Theology: Notes on the* Book of Church Order *of the Reformed Church In America*, by Allan J. Janssen (2000)
34. *Raising the Dead: Sermons of Howard G. Hageman*, edited by Gregg A. Mast (2000)
35. *Equipping the Saints: The Synod of New York, 1800-2000*, edited by James Hart Brumm (2000)
36. *Forerunner of the Great Awakening*, edited by Joel R. Beeke (2000)
37. *Historical Directory of the Reformed Church in America, 1628-2000*, by Russell L. Gasero (2001)
38. *From Mission to Church: The Reformed Church in America in India*, by Eugene Heideman (2001)
39. *Our School: Calvin College and the Christian Reformed Church*, by Harry Boonstra (2001)

40. *The Church Speaks, 2*, edited by James I. Cook (2002)
41. *Concord Makes Strength*, edited by John W. Coakley (2002)
42. *Dutch Chicago: A History of the Hollanders in the Windy City*, by Robert P. Swierenga (2002)
43. *Doctors for the Kingdom*, Paul Armerding (2003)
44. *By Grace Alone*, Donald J. Bruggink (2004)
45. *Travels of an American Girl*, June Potter Durkee (2004)
46. *Letters to Hazel*, Mary Kansfield (2004)
47. *Iowa Letters*, Robert P. Swierenga (2004)
48. *Can Hope Endure, A Historical Case Study in Christian Higher Education*, James C. Kennedy and Caroline J. Simon (2005)
49. *Elim*, Robert P. Swierenga (2005)
50. *Taking the Jesus Road*, LeRoy Koopman (2005)
51. *The Netherlands Reformed Church, 1571-2005*, Karel Blei (2005)
52. *Son of Secession: Douwe J. Vander Werp*, Janet Sjaarda Sheeres (2006)
53. *Kingdom, Office, and Church: A Study of A. A. van Ruler's Doctrine of Ecclesiastical Office*, Allan J. Janssen (2006)
54. *Divided by a Common Heritage: The Christian Reformed Church and the Reformed Church in America at the Beginning of the New Millenium*, Corwin Smidt, Donald Luidens, James Penning, and Roger Nemeth (2006)
55. *Henry J. Kuiper: Shaping the Christian Reformed Church, 1907-1962*, James A. De Jong (2007)
56. *A Goodly Heritage, Essays in Honor of the Reverend Dr. Elton J. Bruins at Eighty*, Jacob E. Nyenhuis (2007)
57. *Liturgy among the Thorns: Essays on Worship in the Reformed Church in America*, James Hart Brumm (2007)
58. *Old Wing Mission*, Robert P. Swierenga (2008)
59. *Herman J. Ridder: Contextual Preacher and President*, edited by George Brown, Jr. (2009)

60. *Tools for Understanding*, edited by James Hart Brumm (2009) 404 pp. ISBN: 978-0-8028-6483-3

"Beginning with Donald Bruggink's own notion that 'history is a tool for understanding,' the dozen essays in this volume are tools for understanding four areas of his life and his fifty-five years of ministry. While all the contributors to this volume have benefited from Bruggink's friendship, teaching, and ministry, the first and last essays are by the contributors he has known longest, who had a formative role in his life"

– Eugene Heideman and I. John Hesselink.

61. *Chinese Theological Education*, edited by Marvin D. Hoff (2009) 470 pp. ISBN: 978-0-8028-6480-2

This book offers insight into the emergence of the Christian church after Mao's Cultural Revolution. While reports of Communist oppression have dominated American perceptions of church and state in China, this is an increasingly dangerous view as China changes. Dr. Marvin D. Hoff, as executive director for the Foundation for Theological Education in Southeast Asia, traveled at least annually to China for the period covered by this book. The original reports of his encounters with Chinese Christians, especially those involved in theological education, are a historic record of the church's growth—and growing freedom. Interspersed with Hoff's accounts are reports of essays by Chinese and other Asian Christians. Introductory essays are provided by Charles W. Forman of Yale Divinity School, Daniel B. Hays of Calvin College, and Donald J. Bruggink of Western Theological Seminary.

62. *Liber A*, edited by Frank Sypher (2009) 442 pp. ISBN: 978-0-8028-6509-0

Liber A of the Collegiate Church archives contains detailed seventeenth-century records of the Reformed Dutch Church of the City of New York, including correspondence, texts of legal documents, and lists of names of consistory members. Especially significant are records pertaining to the granting in 1696 of the royal charter of incorporation of the Church, and records relating to donations for, and construction of the church building on Garden Street. The full Dutch texts have never before been published.

63. *Aunt Tena, Called to Serve: Journals and Letters of Tena A. Huizenga, Missionary Nurse to Nigeria*, edited by Jacob A. Nyenhuis, Robert P. Swierenga, and Lauren M. Berka (2009) 980 pp. ISBN: 978-0-8028-6515-1

When Tena Huizenga felt the call to serve as a missionary nurse to Africa, she followed that call and served seventeen years at Lupwe, Nigeria, during a pivotal era in world missions. As she ministered to the natives, she recorded her thoughts and feelings in a diary and in countless letters to family and friends--over 350 in her first year alone. Through her eyes, we see the Lupwe mission, Tena's colleagues, and the many native helpers. Aunt Tena (Nigerians called all female missionaries

"Aunt") tells this profoundly human story. Interesting in its own right, the book will also prove invaluable to historians, sociologists, and genealogists as they mine this rich resource.

The extensive letters from Tena's brother Pete offer marvelous insights into the Dutch Reformed subculture of Chicago's West Side. Because his scavenger company later evolved into Waste Management Inc., those letters are especially valuable. Pete's winsome descriptions and witty dialogue with his sister add a Chicago flavor to this book.

64. *The Practice of Piety: The Theology of the Midwestern Reformed Church in America, 1866-1966*, by Eugene P. Heideman (2009) 286 pp. ISBN: 978-0-8028-6551-9

"With the instincts of a historian and the affection of a child of the RCA, Gene Heideman has accessed both Dutch and English sources in order to introduce us to the unique theology and piety of the Midwestern section of our denomination from 1866 to 1966. Through the words of pastors, professors, and parishioners, he has fleshed out the Dutch pilgrims of the 19th century who found their roots in the Netherlands but their fruit in America. Accessing the Dutch language newspaper *De Hope*, and the writings and lectures of a century of Western Seminary professors, the history of the RCA in the Midwest has come alive. This book is a gracious and winsome invitation to its readers and other scholars to dig deeper and understand more fully the theological and ethnic heritage of those who have helped ground our past and thus form our future."

– Gregg A. Mast, president, New Brunswick Theological Seminary

65. *Freedom on the Horizon: Dutch Immigration to America, 1840 to 1940*, by Hans Krabbendam (2009) 432 pp. ISBN: 978-0-8028-6545-8

"It's been eighty years since the last comprehensive study of the Dutch immigrant experience by a Netherlands scholar–Jacob Van Hinte's magisterial *Netherlanders in America* (1928, English translation 1985). It was worth the wait! Krabbendam has a firmer grasp of American history and culture than his predecessor, who spent only seven weeks on a whirlwind tour of a half-dozen Dutch 'colonies' in 1921. Krabbendam earned an M.A. degree in the USA, is widely traveled, versed in American religious culture, and has written the definitive biography of Edward W. Box (2001). *Freedom on the Horizon* focuses on the ultimate meaning of immigration–the process by which one's inherited culture is reshaped into a new Dutch-American identity. 'Only the steeple was retained,'

Krabbendam notes in his tale of a congregation that tore down its historic church edifice in favor of a modern new one. This is a metaphor of the Dutch immigrant experience writ large, as told here in a masterful way."

– Robert D. Swierenga, Kent State University

66. *A Collegial Bishop? Classis and Presbytery at Issue*, edited by Allan Janssen and Leon Vanden Broek (2010) 176 pp. ISBN: 978-0-8028-6585-4

In *A Collegial Bishop?* classis and presbytery are considered from a cross-cultural, indeed cross-national, perspective of the inheritors of Geneva and Edinburgh in their contemporary contexts in the Netherlands, South Africa, and the United States.

"Dutch theologian A. A. van Ruler compares church order to the rafters of a church building. Church order sustains the space within which the church is met by God, where it engages in its plan with God (liturgy), and where it is used by God in its mission in and to God's world. Presbyterian church order intends to be faithful to its root in God's Word, as it is shaped around the office of elder and governed through a series of councils of the church."

Alan Janssen
– Pastor, Community Church of Glen Rock, NJ

67. *The Church Under the Cross*, by Wendell Karssen (2010) 454 pp. ISBN: 978-0-8028-6614-1

The Church Under the Cross: Mission in Asia in Times of Turmoil is the illustrated two-volume account of Wendell Paul Karsen's more than three decades of cross-cultural missionary work in East Asia.

In one sense a missionary memoir of Karsen's life and ministry in Taiwan, Hong Kong, China, and Indonesia, the work also chronicles the inspiring story of the Christian communities Karsen served–churches which struggled to grow and witness under adverse circumstances throughout years of political turbulence and social upheaval.

68. *Supporting Asian Christianity's Transition from Mission to Church: A History of the Foundation for Theological Education in Southeast Asia*, edited by Samuel C. Pearson (2010) 464 pp. ISBN: 978-0-8028-6622-6

"This volume, telling the story of how one North American ecumenical foundation learned to move from a 'missions' stance to one of 'partnership,' is at once informative, intriguing, and instructive for anyone curious about or interested in the development of contextual theological education and scholarship in China and Southeast Asia. It traces the efforts of Protestant churches and educational institutions emerging from World War II, revolution, and colonization to train an indigenous leadership and to nurture theological scholars for the political, cultural, and religious realities in which these ecclesial bodies find themselves."

– Greer Anne Wenh-In Ng, Professor Emerita, Victoria University in the University of Toronto

69. *The American Diary of Jacob Van Hinte*, edited by Peter Ester, Nella Kennedy, Earl Wm. Kennedy (2010) 210 pp. ISBN: 978-0-8028-6661-5

"This is a charming translation, scrupulously annotated, of the long-lost travel diary of Jacob Van Hinte (1889–1948), author of the monumental Netherlanders in America. Van Hinte's energetic five-week sprint in the summer of 1921 from "Dutch" Hoboken up the river by dayliner to Albany and on to the Dutch-settled towns and cities in the Midwest convinced him that the "migration to America had been a blessing" to the Dutch. But in his brief sojourn among the descendants of the immigrant generation, he also became aware of the "tales of misery" and the "noble struggles" of the settlers that will put readers of all ethnic backgrounds to wondering about their own poignant histories."

– Firth Fabend, author of Zion on the Hudson: Dutch new York and the New Jersey in the Age of Revivals

70. *A New Way of Belonging: Covenant Theology, China and the Christian Reformed Church, 1921-1951*, by Kurt Selles (2011) 288 pp. ISBN: 978-0-8028-6662-2

"As someone who spent much of my childhood on the mission field described in this book, I anticipated having my early memories refreshed by reading it. I did indeed find the book to be an accurate and thorough account of the work of the CRC China Mission as I remember it, but—more surprising—I also learned a good deal of new information. Kurt Selles has performed an important service for the history of missions by uncovering so much new information and doing such impressive research under difficult circumstances. Although the events took place more than a half-century ago, Selles has been able to retrieve a vast amount of detail. His analysis of the cross-cultural dynamics of this work is insightful. Anyone interested in the successes and failures of Christian mission should find this study interesting and informative."

– J. William Smit, professor of sociology, Calvin College, child of CRC China missionary Albert Smit

71. *Envisioning Hope College: Letters Written by Albertus C. Van Raalte to Philip Phelps, Jr., 1857-1875*, edited by Elton J. Bruins and Karen G. Schakel (2011) 556 pp. ISBN: 978-0-8028-6688-2

These letters between the colony's leader and the first president of Hope College in Holland, Michigan, are sequentially placed in historical context and richly footnoted. They offer an intimate view of Van Raalte as he seeks funding for his college from the Dutch Reformed Church in the east, as well as insights into his pioneer community in the midst of conflagration and war.

72. *Ministry Among the Maya*, by Dorothy Dickens Meyerink (Dec. 2011) 434 pp. ISBN: 978-0-8028-6744-5

Dorothy Meyerink entered her ministry among the Maya of Chiapas, Mexico, in 1956, and spent her entire service there. *Ministry Among the Maya* is an exciting account of persecution and success, relating the story of how, through the faithful witness of the laity and the early ordination of Mayan ministers, a strong, large, indigenous church was established and continues to flourish. Meyerink interweaves her personal experiences and the history of the church with reflections on the effective application of church growth principles.

73. *The Church Under the Cross, Vol. 2*, by Wendell Karsen (Dec. 2011) 802 pp. ISBN: 978-0-8028-6760-5

See volume 67.

74. *Sing to the Lord a New Song: Choirs in the Worship and Culture of the Dutch Reformed Church in America, 1785-1860*, by David M.Tripold (2012) 304 pp. ISBN: 978-0-8028-6874-9

As their privileged status evaporated in America's melting pot, the Dutch Reformed Church was forced to compete with a host of rising Protestant denominations in the New World. Survival became linked to assimilating within a new American way of life, with its own distinct language, culture, and religious practices. Gradually, organs, hymns and institutional church choirs were added to the traditional singing of the Psalter—innovations that altered the very fabric of Dutch Reformed religious life in America.

Sing to the Lord a New Song examines how choirs in particular revolutionized the Dutch Reformed Church in the nineteenth century, transforming the church's very nature in terms of worship, ecclesiastical life, institutional structures, and even social, fiscal, and moral practices. Moreover, the book examines how choirs helped break social barriers, particularly those regarding the status and role of women in the church.

Includes audio CD.

75. *Pioneers to Partners, The Reformed Church in America and Christian Mission to the Japanese*, by Gordon Laman (2012) ISBN: 978-0-8028-6965-4

Beginning with Japan's early exposure to Christianity by the very successful Roman Catholic mission to Japan in the sixteenth and seventeenth centuries, and the resultant persecution and prohibition of Christianity, Laman lays the groundwork for understanding the experience of nineteenth-century Protestant missionaries, among whom those of the Reformed Church in America were in the forefront. The early efforts of the Browns, Verbecks, Ballaghs, and Stouts, their failures and successes, are recounted within the cultural and political context of the anti-Western, anti-Christian Japan of the time.

Verbeck's service to the government helped bring about gradual change. The first Protestant church was organized with a vision for ecumenical mission, and during several promising years, churches and mission schools were organized. Reformed Church missionaries encouraged and trained Japanese leaders from the beginning, the first Japanese ministers were ordained in 1877, and the Japanese church soon exhibited a spirit of independence, ushering in an era of growing missionary/Japanese partnership.

The rise of the Japanese empire, a reinvigorated nationalism, and its progression to militarist ultranationalism brought on a renewed anti-Western, anti-Christian reaction and new challenges to both mission and church. With the outbreak of World War II, the Japanese government consolidated all Protestant churches into the Kyodan to facilitate control.

Laman continues the account of Reformed Church partners in mission in Japan in the midst of post-war devastation and subsequent social and political tensions. The ecumenical involvement and continued clarification of mutual mission finds the Reformed Church a full participant with a mature Japanese church.

76. *Transatlantic Pieties*, ed by Hans Krabbendam, Leon van den Broeke, and Dirk Mouw (2012) 359 pp. ISBN: 978-0-8028-6972-2

Transatlantic Pieties: Dutch Clergy in Colonial America explores the ways in which the lives and careers of fourteen Dutch Reformed ministers illuminate important aspects of European and American colonial society of their times. Based on primary sources, this collection reexamines some of the movers and shakers over the course of 250 years. The essays shed light on the high and low tides, the promises and disappointments, and the factors within and beyond the control of a new society in the making. The portraits humanize and contextualize the lives of these men who served not only as religious leaders and cultural mediators in colonial communities, but also as important connective tissue in the Dutch Atlantic world.

77. *Loyalty and Loss, the Reformed Church in America, 1945-1994*, by Lynn Japinga (2013) ISBN: 978-0-8028-7068-1

Offering a meticulously researched yet also deeply personal history of the Reformed Church in America throughout much of the twentieth century, Lynn Japinga's *Loyalty and Loss* will be of intense interest to the members of the RCA, reminding them of where they have come from, of the bonds that have held them together, and of the many conflicts and challenges that they have together faced and ultimately surmounted.

For those outside the RCA the questions of identity raised by this book will often sound very familiar, especially, perhaps, in its account of the church's struggle throughout recent decades to reconcile the persistently ecumenical spirit of many of its members with the desire of others within the denomination to preserve a real or imagined conservative exclusivity. Others may find the conflicts within the RCA reflective of their own experiences, especially as they relate to such issues as denominational mergers, abortion, the Viet Nam war, and women's ordination.

78. *Oepke Noordmans: Theologian of the Holy Spirit*, Karel Blei (tran. By Allan Janssen) (2013) ISBN: 978-0-8028-7085-8

Oepke Noordmans was one of the major Dutch theologians of

the twentieth century, whose recovery of a vital doctrine of the Holy Spirit placed him at the center of thought on the nature of the church and its ministry.

In this volume Karel Blei, himself a theological voice of note, has provided a lucid introduction to and summary of Noordmans's thought and contextual impact. The book also includes substantial excerpts of Noordmans's writing in translation, offering a compact representation of his work to an English-speaking audience.

79. *The Not-So-Promised Land, The Dutch in Amelia County, Virginia, 1868-1880*, by Janet Sjaarda Sheeres (2013) 248 pp. ISBN: 978-0-8028-7156-5

The sad story of a little-known, short-lived Dutch immigrant settlement.

After establishing a successful Dutch colony in Holland, Michigan, in 1847, Albertus Van Raalte turned his attention to the warmer climes of Amelia County, Virginia, where he attempted to establish a second colony. This volume by Janet Sheeres presents a carefully researched account of that colonization attempt with a thorough analysis of why it failed. Providing insights into the risks of new settlements that books on successful colonies overlook, this is the first major study of the Amelia settlement.

A well-told tale of high hopes but eventual failure, *The Not-So-Promised Land* concludes with a 73-page genealogy of everyone involved in the settlement, including their origins, marriages, births, deaths, denominations, occupations, and post-Amelia destinations.

80. *Holland Michigan, From Dutch Colony to Dynamic City* (3 volumes), by Robert P. Swierenga (2013) ISBN: 978-0-8028-7137-4

Holland Michigan: From Dutch Colony to Dynamic City is a fresh and comprehensive history of the city of Holland from its beginnings to the increasingly diverse community it is today.

The three volumes that comprise this monumental work discuss such topics as the coming of the Dutch, the Americans who chose to live among them, schools, grassroots politics, the effects of the world wars and the Great Depression, city institutions, downtown renewal, and social and cultural life in Holland. Robert Swierenga also draws attention to founder Albertus Van Raalte's particular role in forming the city—everything from planning streets to establishing churches and schools, nurturing industry, and encouraging entrepreneurs.

Lavishly illustrated with nine hundred photographs and based on meticulous research, this book offers the most detailed history of Holland, Michigan, in print.

The volume received the Historical Society of Michigan 2014 State History Award in the Books, University and Commercial Press category

81. *The Enduring Legacy of Albertus C. Van Raalte as Leader and Liaison*, edited by Jacob E. Nyenhuis and George Harinck (2013) 560 pp. ISBN: 978-0-8028-7215-9

The celebration of the bicentennial of the birth of Albertus C. Van Raalte in October 2011 provided a distinct opportunity to evaluate the enduring legacy of one of the best-known Dutch immigrants of the nineteenth century. This book of essays demonstrates his unique role not only in the narrative of the migration to America but also in the foundation of theological education for Seceders (Afgescheidenen) prior to his emigration. These essays were all presented at an international conference held in Holland, Michigan, and Ommen, Overijssel, the Netherlands, with the conference theme of "Albertus C. Van Raalte: Leader and Liaison." Three broad categories serve as the organizing principle for this book: biographical essays, thematic essays, and reception studies.

Van Raalte began to emerge as a leader within the Seceder Church (Christelijk Afgescheidene Gereformeerde Kerk) in the Netherlands, but his leadership abilities were both tested and strengthened through leading a group of Dutch citizens to the United States in 1846. In his role as leader, moreover, he served as liaison to the Reformed Protestant Dutch Church in America in the eastern United States (renamed the Reformed Church in America in 1867) to the Seceder Church in the Netherlands, and to the civil authorities in the United States, as well as between business and their employees.

These fifteen essays illuminate the many facets of this energetic, multi-talented founder of the Holland kolonie. This collection further enhances and strengthens our knowledge of both Van Raalte and his Separatist compatriots.

82. *Minutes of the Christian Reformed Church, Classical Assembly, 1857-1870, General Assembly, 1867-79, and Synodical Assembly, 1880*, edited and annotated by Janet Sjaarda Sheeres (2014) 668 pp. ISBN: 978-0-8028-7253-1

"Janet Sheeres, noted scholar of the Dutch in North America, here turns her skill to the early years of the Christian Reformed Church in North America. She has painstakingly researched all the individuals who attended denominational leadership gatherings and the issues discussed and debated at these meetings. Her extensive annotations to a new translation of the minutes provides unprecedented and cogent insight into the early years of the denomination and the larger Dutch trans-Appalachian immigration of the nineteenth century. The annotations reflect Sheeres's characteristically detailed research in both Dutch and English. Scholars of immigration, religion, Dutch-American immigrants, and the Christian Reformed Church will benefit from data in this book, and the appendix of biographical data will be invaluable to those interested in family research."

– Richard Harms, archivist of the Christian Reformed Church

83 *New Brunswick Theological Seminary: an Illustrated History, 1784-2014.* John W. Coakley (2014) ISBN: 978-0-8028-7296-8

This volume marks the 230th anniversary of New Brunswick Theological Seminary and the reconfiguring of its campus by retelling the school's history in text and pictures. John Coakley, teacher of church history at the seminary for thirty years, examines how the mission of the school has evolved over the course of the seminary's history, focusing on its changing relationship to the community of faith it has served in preparing men and women for ministry.

In four chapters representing four significant eras in the seminary's history, Coakley traces the relationship between the seminary in New Brunswick and the Reformed Church in America, showing that both the seminary and the RCA have changed dramatically over the years but have never lost each other along the way.

84. *Hendrik P. Scholte: His Legacy in the Netherlands and in America.* Eugene P. Heideman (2015) 314 pp. ISBN: 978-0-8028-7352-1

This book offers a careful contextual theological analysis of a nineteenth-century schismatic with twenty-first-century ecumenical intent.

Hendrik P. Scholte (1803-1868) was the intellectual leader and catalyst of a separation from the Nederlandse Hervormde Kerk. Leaving the state church meant being separated from its deacon's funds, conflict with the laws of the state, and social ostracism. Due to poverty, Scholte emigrated with a group that settled Pella, Iowa. Schismatic tendencies continued in this and other nineteenth-century Dutch settlements with the most notable division being between those who joined the

Reformed Church in America and those who became the Christian Reformed Church in North America.

As Heideman says: "Although this book concentrates on what happened in the past, it is written with the hope that knowledge of the past will contribute to the faithfulness and unity of the church in the future."

85. *Liber A:1628-1700 of the Collegiate Churches of New York, Part 2,* translated, annotated, and edited by Frank J. Sypher, Jr. (2015) 911 pp. ISBN: 978-0-8028-7341-5

See volume 62.

86. *KEMP: The Story of John R. and Mabel Kempers, Founders of the Reformed Church in America Mission in Chiapas, Mexico,* by Pablo A. Deiros. 558 pp. ISBN 978-0-8028-7354-5

"This faithful story reveals God's power to transform thousands of people's lives through a couple committed to spreading God's message of love and devotion. The Kempers' commitment to their slogan "Chiapas para Cristo" was evidenced in all that they did. They were our surrogate parents, mission colleagues, and mentors."

– Sam and Helen Hofman, career RCA missionaries in Chiapas, Mexico.

"Employing a creative narrative style, Pablo Deiros has fashioned a fully documented biography into a compelling story of the lives and witness of John and Mabel Kempers. *Kemp* is a must read for those who are interested in the intersection of the Christian Church and the social revolution in Mexico during the twentieth century, the struggles of Maya cultures in Chiapas, and the transformative impact of the gospel of Jesus Christ among the people of Chiapas. *Kemp* is an inspiring and engaging history."

– Dennis N. Voskuil, Director, Van Raalte Institute

87. *Yes! Well...Exploring the Past, Present, and Future of the Church: Essays in Honor of John W. Coakley,* edited by James Hart Brumm. 324pp. ISBN: 978-0-8028-7479-5

In this volume, authors from around the world present essays in honor of John W. Coakley, L. Russell Feakes Memorial Professor Emeritus of Church History at New Brunswick Theological Seminary in

New Jersey. Following the pattern of Coakley's teaching, the contributors push readers to think about aspects of the church in new ways.

Contributors include: Thomas A. Boogart, James Hart Brumm, Kathleen Hart Brumm, Jaeseung Cha, James F. Coakley, Sarah Coakley. Matthew Gasero, Russell Gasero, Allan Janssen, Lynn Japinga, Mary L. Kansfield, Norman J. Kansfield, James Jinhong Kim, Gregg A. Mast, Dirk Mouw, Ondrea Murphy, Mark V. C. Taylor, and David W. Waanders

88. *Elephant Baseball: A Missionary Kids Tale*, by Paul Heusinkveld. 282 pp. ISBN: 978-0-8028-7550-1

This fascinating book recounts the up-and-down experiences of a missionary kid growing up overseas away from home in the 1960s. A sensitive autobiographical exploration of the universal trials of adolescence, Paul Heusinkveld's *Elephant Baseball* luxuriates in narrative fluidity—truly a riveting read.

89. Growing Pains: How Racial Struggles Changed a Church and a School, by Christopher H. Meehan. 240 pp. ISBN: 978-0-80287-570-9

In the 1960s, black parents from Lawndale Christian Reformed Church in Chicago tried to enroll their children in an all-white Christian school in the suburb of Cicero. A power struggle ensued, taking the matter to synod and inspiring the creation of the Office of Race Relations.

90. *A Ministry of Reconciliation: Essays in Honor of Gregg Mast*, edited by Allan J. Janssen. 272 pp. ISBN: 978-0-80287-598-3

Respect and affection for Gregg Mast permeates this volume of essays written by his colleagues across the fruitful years of his ministry. He certainly has much to show for his years of labor; the list of his accomplishments is long. But it is his heart that impresses me the most. I consider it a privilege to number myself as one of his colleagues, and I can attest, along with many others, to his generosity of spirit, kindness of speech, and faithful persistence of character. This book is a fitting tribute to his impact, and I warmly commend it to a wide readership.

Leanne Van Dyk
President and Professor of Theology
Columbia Theological Seminary
Decatur, Georgia

91. *For Better, For Worse: Stories of the Wives of Early Pastors of the Christian Reformed Church*, by Janet Sjaarda Sheeres. 224 pp. ISBN: 978-0-80287-625-6

In *For Better, for Worse*, Janet Sjaarda Sheeres highlights the lives of the wives of the first ten pastors of the Christian Reformed Church. Beginning in 1857, when the CRC was founded, Sheeres proceeds in the order in which the first ten pastors joined the church.

Drawing on genealogical and census data, church records from congregations their husbands served, and historical information about the position of women at the time, Sheeres brings the untold stories of these women's lives to light.

92. *In Peril on the Sea: The Forgotten Story of the William & Mary Shipwreck*, by Kenneth A. Schaaf. 382 pp. ISBN: 978-0-98914-696-8

"Historian Ken Schaaf has mined the rich holdings of the Library of Congress, the National Archives, and research facilities on both sides of the Atlantic to uncover the amazing story of the eighty-six Frisians who boarded the William & Mary en route to America. After weeks of sailing, they found themselves abandoned at sea by captain and crew aboard their sinking vessel. Readers interested in transatlantic passages under sail will not be able to put this book down. The story grabs the emotions and will not let go."

—Robert P. Swierenga, Senior Research Fellow,
Van Raalte Institute

93. *Jack: A Compassionate Compendium: A Tribute to Dr. Jacob E. Nyenhuis, Scholar, Servant, Leader*, edited by Donald A. Luidens and JoHannah M. Smith. 366 pp. ISBN: 978-0-98914-697-5

A tribute to Dr Jacob E. Nyenhuis, scholar, servant, and leader. Nyenhuis served as a professor of Classics at Hope College (Holland, Michigan) and later served as its Provost, before becoming the director of the Van Raalte Institute.

94. *A Commentary on the Minutes of the Classis of Holland, 1848-1876: A Detailed Record of Persons and Issues, Civil and Religious, in the Dutch Colony of Holland, Michigan*, edited by Earl William Kennedy (three volumes). 2,080 pp. ISBN: 978-0-98914-695-1

"This much-anticipated, annotated edition in English of the Dutch-language minutes of the Classis of Holland (Michigan)—the seminal regional assembly of Dutch Reformed immigrants in the Midwest—is extraordinary for its scope and detail. Every substantive theological and ecclesiastical issue, whether Netherlandic or American in origin, is rooted in the foundational Synod of Dort (1618-19) and the Later (Nadere) Reformation. In addition, Kennedy provides biographical sketches of virtually every ministerial and elder delegate, likely hundreds of churchmen. Only a scholar grounded in Reformed theological and ecclesiastical history, fluent in languages, and skilled in genealogical search engines could have written such an extensive work. This multivolume sourcebook will be indispensable to anyone interested in Reformed church history."

—Robert P Swierenga, Research Professor, A. C. Van Raalte Institute, Hope College

95. *Hope College at 150: Anchored in Faith, Educating for Leadership and Service in a Global Society*, Jacob Nyenhuis et alii (two volumes).1,414pp. ISBN: 978-1-950572-00-7

A comprehensive survey and history of 150 years of Hope College, edited by Jack Nyenhuis with contributions by James C. Kennedy, Dennis N. Voskuil, Robert P. Swierenga, Alfredo M. Gonzales, John E. Jobson, Michael J. Douma, Thomas L. Renner, and Scott Travis. The two volume set includes many full-color images of the buildings on the campus and the history of Hope's architecture as well as lists of alumni, faculty, enrollment data, summaries of student life and housing, ending with a plan for the future.

96. Remembrance, Communion, and Hope: Essays in Honor of Allan J. Janssen, edited by Matthew J. van Maastricht, 261 pp., ISBN: 978-1-9505-7201-4

This festschrift in honor of Allan Janssen's service as a General Synod Professor looks at his work as a theologian, ecclesiologist, and polity expert, who was, first and foremost, a pastor and teacher. Featuring essays by Carol M. Bechtel, Abraham van de Beek, Karel Blei, Leon van den Broeke, John W. Coakley, Daniel M. Griswold, Eugene P. Heideman, Paul Janssen, Leo J. Koffeman, Christo Lombard, Matthew J. van Maastricht, Gregg Mast, Daniel J. Meeter, and Micah L. McCreary.

97. Before the Face of God: Essays in Honor of Tom Boogaart, edited by Dustyn Elizabeth Keepers, 336 pages, ISBN: 978-1950572021

A collection of essays in honor of the long-time professor of Old Testament at Western Theological Seminary on the occasion of his retirement, including works by Jeff Barker, Carol M. Bechtel, Tim Brown, James Brownson, Pam Bush, John W, Coakley, Benjamin Conner, Christopher Dorn, Jaco J. Hamman, Christopher B. Kaiser, Dustyn Elizabeth Keepers, Zac Poppen, Alberto La Rosa Rojas, Kyle Small, David L. Stubbs, Lyle VanderBroek, Travis West, and Stephen J. Wykstra. 96. *Remembrance, Communion, and Hope: Essays in Honor of Allan J. Janssen*, edited by Matthew J. van Maastricht, 261 pp., ISBN: 978-1-9505-7201-4

This festschrift in honor of Allan Janssen's service as a General Synod Professor looks at his work as a theologian, ecclesiologist, and polity expert, who was, first and foremost, a pastor and teacher. Featuring essays by Carol M. Bechtel, Abraham van de Beek, Karel Blei, Leon van den Broeke, John W. Coakley, Daniel M. Griswold, Eugene P. Heideman, Paul Janssen, Leo J. Koffeman, Christo Lombard, Matthew J. van Maastricht, Gregg Mast, Daniel J. Meeter, and Micah L. McCreary.

98. A Constant State of Emergency: Paul de Kruif, Microbe Hunter and Health Activist, by Jan Peter Verhave, 656 pages, ISBN: 978-1-950572-06-9

A biography of the Dutch Reformed health care champion whose influence on the fields of immunology, medicine, and microbiology in the mid-twentieth century was world-changing. De Kruif fought for the reform of the American health care system, the presentation and treatment of diseases, and affordable health care for all.

99. Register of Marriages from 1783 to 1905 in the Collegiate Churches of New York, edited by Francis J. Sypher, Jr., 447 pages, ISBN: 978-1-9505-7203-8

Meticulously transcribed and annotated records of the oldest Protestant congregations with a continuous ministry in North America, providing invaluable data to church members, genealogists, biographers, social historians, demographers, and anyone curious about people in New York through the eighteenth to twentieth centuries.

100. Constitutional Theology: Notes on the book of Church Order of the Reformed Church in America, second edition, by Allan J. Janssen, 328 pages, ISBN: 978-1950572045

This is the updated, second edition by one of the RCAs foremost researchers. The volume offers commentary that explains the proper roles of elders, deacons, classes, and synods and details the procedures necessary for successful church life. Based on the Book of Church

Order, this helpful volume will assist church leaders in their callings and prevent the myriad difficulties that arise when appropriate procedures are not followed. A necessity for every pastor, elder, and deacon.

101. The Church Remembers: Papers of the RCA Commission on History, 1977 to 2019, edited by James Hart Brumm, 174 pages, ISBN: 978-1-9505-7211-3

A collection of seventeen papers presented by the Commission on History covering the historical development of the Constitution of the Reformed Church in America, the General Synod, RCA Ecclesiology, and the relationship of the Church to the world. These papers look at events from the sixteenth century Reformation to the present, always with an eye toward how these past events inform the present and future work of the church.

102. Called to Serve: Essays on RCA Global Mission, edited by Charles Van Engen, Jean Van Engen, and Sally Tapley, 162 pages, ISBN: 978-1-9505-7213-7

A collection of brief a=essays primarily my missionaries who worked in the field, sharing stories of this work that is integral to the fabric of the Reformed Church in America and giving readers a glimpse of faithful people doing their best to follow God. Contributors include Alan Beagley, Jeanette Beagley-Koolhaas, James Hart Brumm, William DeBoer, Lind Walvoord deVelder, Eugene Heidemann, J. Samuel Hoffman, John Hubers, Derrick Jones, LeRoy Koopman, Gordon D. Laman, Jacob Moss, Richard Otterness, Sally Tapley, Carles E. Van Engen, and Jean Van Engen.

www.ingramcontent.com/pod-product-compliance
Lightning Source LLC
Chambersburg PA
CBHW070757100426
42742CB00012B/2176

* 9 7 8 1 9 5 0 5 7 2 1 7 5 *